Here's what people are saying about
DISARMING SCRIPTURE...

"A perceptive and honest book about the vexed question of violence in the Bible. Taking with great seriousness the dynamism of the biblical tradition and the interpretive process, the distinctive contribution of *Disarming Scripture* is an exploration of the way in which the biblical text itself interprets texts of violence. This is a fine contribution to our common work."

Walter Brueggemann
Emeritus professor, Columbia Theological Seminary
and author of *The Prophetic Imagination*

"In *Disarming Scripture*, Derek Flood shows us how we can confront the many difficult passages in the Bible which seem to condone or even command violence—by reading and understanding Scripture the same way that Jesus did. I recommend this book to anyone who seeks to reconcile the violence of the Old Testament with Jesus' commandment to love our enemies."

Jim Wallis
president of Sojourners
New York Times bestselling author of *The UnCommon Good*

"Jesus is the savior of everything—including the Bible! That's what I kept thinking while reading this brilliant book. There have been a number of excellent books in recent years on how Christians should read the Bible, but *Disarming Scripture* is the very best. Derek has done us an immeasurable service in showing us how to read the Bible like Jesus did."

Brian Zahnd
Pastor of Word of Life Church
and author of *A Farewell to Mars*

"A morally responsible, dynamic reading of scripture, where Jesus and Paul move us along a trajectory toward a non-violent God and a non-violent people of God. Flood leaves no stone unturned in presenting his case with remarkable subtlety in an easy-reading style, handling biblical violence with bracing honesty and spiritual and intellectual substance."

Peter Enns,
Professor of Biblical Studies, Eastern University,
and author of *The Bible Tells Me So*

"*Disarming Scripture* may well be the most thought-provoking and liberating book about the Bible that you will ever read. How do we reconcile a God of grace and compassion with the one who sanctions violence and killing? Far from shying away from these and many other important questions, Derek Flood demonstrates not only how the prophets and Jesus himself often questioned scripture—but shows us why we have a responsibility to do exactly the same."

Steve Chalke MBE
Founder, Oasis Global and Stop The Traffik
and Author of *The Lost Message of Jesus*

This book is a breath of fresh air! *Disarming Scripture* is a marvelous resource for those troubled by how the Bible has been used to justify violence and to harm others. Engaging, informative, compelling, and desperately needed. Highly recommended!"

Eric A. Seibert
Professor of Old Testament, Messiah College
and author of *The Violence of Scripture*

"Of the many recent books on the problem of divinely sanctioned violence in the Bible, Disarming Scripture is one of the most accessible and practically helpful. In wonderfully clear prose, Derek confronts the problem of a violent God in

Scripture, and its baleful legacy in Christian history, with unflinching honesty, demonstrating the kind of hermeneutical sophistication required to make sense of the Bible's dissonant voices. Enormously helpful in charting a middle way between those who prioritize the authority of the text over its morality, and those who jettison the text out of moral indignation over its content."

Christopher D. Marshall
Diana Unwin Chair in Restorative Justice
Victoria University of Wellington, N.Z.

"How do we faithfully follow Christ, yet take seriously the "toxic texts" of Scripture? What of the competing images of God—now restorative, now merciless—within the Bible? *Disarming Scripture* cuts through the unquestioning obedience and cynical dismissiveness of conservative and liberal alike, wading into the issues fearlessly, seriously and creatively. Clear-minded and accessible. A keeper, but not to yourself!"

Brad Jersak
Faculty of NT and Patristics
Westminster Theological Centre

"Fresh and insightful with profound implications for how we read the Bible! There are not enough superlatives to describe *Disarming Scripture*. Derek believes that questioning the text, rather than living in blind obedience to it, is actually the highest form of faithfulness. I think he's right. As a matter of fact, I think he's so right that *Disarming Scripture* has moved to the top of my list of best books on understanding the Bible!"

Raborn Johnson,
co-host of www.beyondtheboxpodcast.com

"Respecting and honoring scripture must entail the integrity to engage it honestly. *Disarming Scripture* takes us on that journey and opens the way for a powerful encounter with these ancient texts.

Both engaging the violence in the texts and pointing to compassion-informed ways of dealing with such violence and its impacts, *Disarming Scripture* points to new possibilities for a mature Christian approach to the Bible."

William Loader,
Murdoch University, and author of
Jesus and the Fundamentalism of His Day

DISARMING SCRIPTURE

DISARMING
SCRIPTURE

Cherry-Picking Liberals,
Violence-Loving Conservatives,
and Why We All Need to Learn
to Read the Bible Like Jesus Did

Derek Flood

 Metanoia Books, San Francisco

DISARMING SCRIPTURE
Cherry-Picking Liberals, Violence-Loving Conservatives, and Why We All
Need to Learn to Read the Bible Like Jesus Did

Metanoia Books
180 Stewart Street #193065
San Francisco, CA 94119

ISBN: 978-0-692-30726-7
eISBN: 978-0-692-30727-4

Library of Congress Cataloging in-publication data:

Flood, Derek

    Disarming scripture: cherry-picking liberals, violence-loving conservatives,
and why we all need to learn to read the Bible like Jesus did / Derek Flood.
    pages cm. —Includes bibliographical references.
    ISBN 978-0-692-30726-7 (pbk.)
    ISBN: 978-0-692-30727-4 (e-book)
    1. Ethics in the Bible 2. Violence—Biblical teaching. 3. Bible—Criticism,
Interpretation, etc. 4. Bible—Hermeneutics. 5. Evangelicalism. I. Title.

BS480.F56 2014
220.1—dc23

                                       2014918605

Manufactured in the USA

For Julia, my sister-soul

CONTENTS

FOREWORD

You need Derek Flood. You need his intelligence. You need his faithfulness. You need his courage. You need his insight. You need his message in this book. So do I.

Here's why.

In the aftermath of September 11, 2001, more and more people are concerned about the linkage between religion and violence—especially when holy texts, whether the Quran or the Bible, are brought in to justify attack and revenge, torture and killing.

As we witness, in our lifetimes, hundreds of thousands of dead or damaged human beings ... children, grandparents, women, and men killed or bereaved, dispossessed or marginalized ... fewer and fewer of us are willing to affiliate with forms of religion that are used to bolster hatred and hostility.

It's not an exaggeration to say that the future of the planet depends in large measure on our success in disarming our sacred texts.

Many of us who are Christians are growing increasingly uncomfortable with the way some Christians use the Bible to defend and promote violence. We squirm and wince when we hear "Onward, Christian Soldiers," or when popular televangelists urge politicians to "blow them all away in the name of the Lord." We want to put the safety on the gun, so to speak, to disarm the ticking time bomb—to turn the sword into a plowshare. We want to find a way of reading the Bible that sends us into the world as peacemakers, reconcilers, bridge-builders, neighbor- and even enemy-lovers.

You probably don't know Derek's name yet. But you won't forget it after you read this book. You might not agree with everything Derek says here. But after giving this book a thoughtful read, you probably won't agree with everything you have always said and thought either.

Millions of people have been helped in millions of ways by reading the Bible in exactly the way that Derek exposes to critical thinking in this text. They have gained from the Bible reasons to get and stay married, to love their parents and children, to be good neighbors and honest employees, to avoid stealing and lying and cheating, and to support their local church. They have gained from the Bible comfort in distress, consolation in loss, and hope in the face of sickness and death.

Understandably, they fear that if they allow themselves to question their way of reading the Bible, all of these and other benefits they and others have gained will be lost to them.

As a result, they are, perhaps without realizing it, willing to allow continuing the "collateral damage" of war, torture, abuse, oppression and death among "them," as long as the long-cherished benefits continue to flow to "us." They want to keep benefitting from the "balm" of the Bible, even if the Bible is used to "bomb" others.

Derek wants to stop the damage to both us and them without losing the legitimate benefits that come from reading the Bible as a holy, God-given, inspired and inspiring text. He won't ask you to throw out the Bible. Not at all: he is offering you a way to keep it—by disarming it.

You may have been told that there are only two ways to read the Bible: a "conservative" way that treats the text as God's words, virtually dictated to humankind ... or a "liberal" way that treats the text with a lot of "nothing buttery"—reducing it to nothing but a human text, nothing but a bunch of moralisms and myths, nothing but primitive superstitions.

If that's what you've been told, you've either been intentionally lied to or unintentionally misinformed, and you're about to discover a vital alternative: reading the Bible ethically, responsibly, wisely, maturely, and faithfully—unafraid to ask questions, but unwilling to "nothing butterize" something as wonderful, revelatory, and rich as the Bible.

Having been Derek's friend and a believer in Derek's work for several years now, I expected this book to be good. But it is even better than expected. One of the ways it surpassed my expectations—Derek's irenic attitude towards those with whom he disagrees. He thus models not only a mind dedicated to disarming Scripture so that it can not so easily be used in harmful ways, but also a heart that is in the lifelong process of being similarly disarmed.

I come from a conservative Christian background. Fundamentalist was a word that people from my church wore as a badge of honor. I remember what it felt like to read a book that questioned some of our "essentials," as we called them. To even leaf through such a book, I would feel a combination of shame and terror ... shame that I might be doing something wrong or sinful, and terror that if I ended up agreeing with the "outsider" book, I would be condemned and excommunicated by my community ... and even worse, labeled with the worst of all possible epithets: liberal.

You may come from a more liberal Christian background, one where conservative was an equal and opposite epithet. In your tribe, preachers only talked about the nice and inspiring bits of the Bible. These they preached, put on calendars and church bulletins, all the while acting as if the other less uplifting parts weren't there at all. Regarding the violent passages in the Bible, there was a "don't ask, don't tell" policy, something suspiciously similar to a cover-up.

Maybe you have gradually dispensed with the Bible altogether, treating it as a primitive and dangerous set of documents we'd be better off leaving in a dusty museum, closed and in a glass box. Yet you suspect that we may be making a mistake in this kind of wholesale dismissal. You wonder if the Bible can be disarmed and recovered.

If you identify with any of these emotions or responses, I want to encourage you all the more to read this book—for two reasons.

First, I believe that you are exactly the kind of person who needs this book and can benefit from it.

Second, I believe that when you are done with this book, you will love the Bible, God, and your faith more, not less, than you do right now.

So, take a deep breath and turn the page. It's time to disarm Scripture.

Brian D. McLaren
brianmclaren.net
Marco Island, Florida

PART I:

VIOLENCE AND THE OLD TESTAMENT

CHAPTER 1

CONFRONTING VIOLENCE
IN SCRIPTURE

Christians have long sought to reconcile the loving God they encounter in the New Testament with the violent and angry depictions of God found in the pages of the Old Testament. On the one hand, Jesus tells us to love our enemies and pray for those who persecute us (Matt 5:44). On the other hand, we read in the law of Moses the divine command for God's people to "show them no mercy" (Deut 7:2) and "kill everything that breathes" (Deut 20:16). Although it may be hard for us to face, such glaring contrasts found within the canon of Scripture are hard to overlook.

Does the Bible describe a God of love or a God of genocide? How are we to reconcile that the apparent answer to this question is that it describes both? As people of faith, we need to face the sobering fact that some parts of our Bible command us to love our enemies, while other parts command mercilessly slaughtering them.[1]

Understandably, this presents a crisis of faith for those of us who regard the Bible as being normative for our lives—who see the Bible as being our own sacred scripture. How are we to make sense of this? If the Bible is God's Word, how can it present such starkly contrasting visions of who God is, and what faithfulness to God entails? What effect does this have on our ability to trust and love God? How does it affect how we see and treat others when such violent passages are meditated upon and internalized as Holy Scripture?

These are obviously not questions that can be sufficiently addressed from an intellectual perspective alone—whether that means the detached perspectives of liberal biblical scholarship or conservative apologetics. These are issues that cut to the heart, that impact our lives in profound ways, and that can have devastating consequences.

---

1   It's important to note that this contrast is not simply between what Christians refer to as the New and Old Testaments. The Hebrew Bible itself contains both messages of compassion and mercy, as well as other passages like the ones above that promote the polar opposite. Similarly, as we will see in later chapters, the New Testament has been used to justify slavery and state violence. So the answer is not as simple as rejecting the Old and focusing on the New, but will require us to go deeper.

The approach taken in this book will therefore be to attempt to honestly wrestle with these questions from a perspective of faith, with the ultimate goal of understanding how Jesus' reading of Scripture led him to a message of radical forgiveness and enemy love, and how adopting his way of reading Scripture can allow us to faithfully confront religious violence as well, rather than seeking either to justify it or explain it away.

The first step in that journey is to begin by taking a long and sobering look at the extent to which human violence is not merely described in the Bible, but actively promoted as God's will. This is not simply a matter of a few troublesome passages. Violence and bloodshed committed in God's name is a major theme of the Old Testament.

The Old Testament records that the Israelites were commanded by God to kill every man, woman, and child in the neighboring nations. Entering into the "promised land" is a story of mass genocide, described in terms of a holy war. "Break down their altars, smash their pillars, hew down their sacred poles, and burn their idols with fire. *For you are a people holy to the LORD your God....* You shall devour all the peoples that the LORD your God is giving over to you, showing them no pity" (Deut 7:5–6, 16).

Elsewhere in the Old Testament, holiness is characterized by compassion and mercy. Here, however, the opposite is the case: Holiness is not understood here in terms of goodness and mercy. On the contrary, it is characterized by a *refusal* of mercy—being "holy" here entails mercilessly committing genocide in God's name.

3

We are faced here with two very different understandings of who God is, two diametrically opposed understandings of what holiness looks like. On the one hand, we have a God of mercy and love, and on the other we encounter a "God of war." In fact, one of the most frequent names for God in the Old Testament, occurring 235 times, is "the Lord of Hosts," which literally means "God of Armies" in Hebrew. As Moses declares, "YAHWEH is a warrior; YAHWEH is his name" (Exod 15:3).

What biblical scholars refer to as the "genocide narrative" is a central theme of the books of both Deuteronomy and Joshua, and constitutes a major component of the defining story of the Israelites as they came into the "promised land." However, such violence is by no means confined to these books. The prophets seem to delight in imagining in disturbing detail the horror that such conquests would have entailed: "Their little ones will be dashed to the ground, their pregnant women ripped open" (Hos 13:16).

Elsewhere, God is repeatedly portrayed as causing parents to cannibalize their own children (Lev 26:29; Jer 19:9; Lam 2:20; Ezek 5:10; Isa 49:25–26). The graphic imagery in these passages is obviously intended to instill appalling fear in a violent God who is either on your side as you kill in his name, or who will inflict the most violent and humiliating suffering on you if you disobey. As the prophet Jeremiah writes:

> You may ask yourself, "Why is all this happening to me?"
> Because of your many sins! That is why you have been

4

stripped and raped by invading armies ... "This is your allotment, the portion I have assigned to you," says the LORD, "For you have forgotten me, putting your trust in false gods. I myself will strip you and expose you to shame!" (Jer 13:22, 25, NLT).

Genocide, infanticide, cannibalism, and rape are all attributed to God in the Old Testament. For those of us who see the Bible as God's Word, this presents a profound problem: How can we say that the Bible is inspired when it seems to approve of, and even command things, that we would in any other context clearly regard as being profoundly immoral?

In his compelling study of violence in the Bible, the late Swiss Roman Catholic priest and theologian Raymund Schwager writes that, "Approximately *one thousand passages* speak of Yahweh's blazing anger, of his punishment by death and destruction, and how like a consuming fire he passes judgment, takes revenge, and threatens annihilation ... No other topic is as often mentioned as God's bloody works."[2] Schwager further states that over 100 passages in the Old Testament cite Yahweh as explicitly commanding people to kill.[3]

In other words, at issue is not simply what God does, but what humans do in God's name. Again, this is by no means a peripheral theme. As Schwager so powerfully illustrates,

---

2   Raymund Schwager, *Must There Be Scapegoats?: Violence and Redemption in the Bible* (San Francisco: Harper & Row, 1987) 55. Emphasis in the original.

3   Schwager, 60.

religiously justified violence is an unavoidable and central theme of the Hebrew Bible. Consider, for example, these two verses:

> This is what the Lord Almighty says ... "Attack the Amalekites ... Do not spare them; put to death men and women, children and infants" (1 Sam 15:2-3).

> O daughter Babylon ... Blessed is the one who seizes your infants and dashes them against the rocks! (Psalm 137:8-9).

Note that these passages are not simply about God judging people. If they were, then we might perhaps argue that God alone has the right to give life and to take it. Here, however, humans are explicitly commanded to kill little children in God's name in 1 Samuel 15, and such acts are said to have God's blessing in Psalm 137.

Likewise, these verses are not simply a record of human atrocity. Again, if they were, we could then perhaps claim that this was a record of human sin, recorded in the Bible as a sober reminder to us. No, these passages are calling for people to kill other people in God's name—to kill toddlers, in fact. In the first verse it is stated as a direct command of God to commit genocide. In the second it is celebrated as having God's blessing to kill little children of an enemy nation as an act of revenge.

A LEGACY OF VIOLENCE

How can we, as Christians, reconcile deeply disturbing passages like these with the God revealed in Jesus who commands us to love our enemies? How can we reconcile the love of God we have come to know in our own lives personally with this brutal and terrifying picture of God recorded in Scripture? These are extremely difficult questions. What makes these questions all the more pertinent is Christianity's long history of violence.

The shocking reality is that these very texts have been used repeatedly by Christians to justify genocides, beginning with the crusades and continuing up to present times. Fighting in the name of Christ, and with crosses emblazoned on their chests, crusaders sacked Jerusalem in 1099, slaughtering the Jewish and Muslim inhabitants, cutting down unarmed men, women and children with the sword.

To this day it is remembered by Muslims as a grave atrocity. According to their own accounts, the crusaders killed 80,000 people in the sack of Jerusalem.[4] Following the massacre, the crusaders sang hymns of thanksgiving. One eyewitness writes in praise of this ghastly event:

> In the Temple and porch of Solomon men rode in blood up
> to their knees and bridle reins. Indeed it was a just and

---

4   F . E. Peters, *Jerusalem: The Holy City in the Eyes of Chroniclers, Visitors, Pilgrims, and Prophets from the Days of Abraham to the Beginnings of Modern Times* (Princeton, NJ: Princeton University Press, 1985) 286–7.

7

splendid judgment of God that this place should be filled with the blood of unbelievers, since it had suffered so long from their blasphemies. The city was filled with corpses and blood.[5]

The heart grows sick to contemplate the horrific reality that this describes, and we may wish to distance ourselves from this violent past. After all, we might be tempted to say, "The crusades happened a long time ago, right?" Sadly, this legacy of violence did not stop with the crusades. Philip Jenkins catalogs how the Old Testament's "conquest narrative" has been used repeatedly to justify violence throughout Western history.[6]

For example, drawing from the deadly logic of Old Testament genocide accounts, Oliver Cromwell described Irish Catholics as modern day "Canaanites," justifying their indiscriminate slaughter with these chilling words: "There are great occasions in which some men are called to great services in the doing of which they are excused from the common rule of morality."[7] Native Americans were likewise frequently cast in the role of the "Canaanites" and "Amalekites" in order to justify their slaughter.

As Sylvester Johnson states, the result of this was that through war, starvation, and disease at least 95% of the 100 million

---

5   Peters, *Jerusalem.* 285–6.

6   Philip Jenkins, *Laying Down the Sword: Why We Can't Ignore the Bible's Violent Verses* (New York: HarperOne, 2011) 124–141.

7   Cited in John J. Collins, "The Zeal of Phinehas: The Bible and the Legitimation of Violence" *JBL* 122/1 (2003) 3-21.

Native Americans were wiped out.[8] As recently as 1994, these same biblical texts were used to spur on the killing of around 800,000 Tutsis in the Rwandan genocide. Inciting his congregation to participate in the massacre, one pastor preached on 1 Samuel 15 where Saul is rejected by God for failing to wipe out the Amalekites:

> "If you don't exterminate the Tutsis you'll be rejected. If you don't want to be rejected by God, then finish the job of killing the people God has rejected. No child, no wife, no old man should be left alive." And the people said, "Amen."[9]

This is the dark side of our Christian history, a history that has been repeatedly justified by an appeal to the biblical genocide accounts, and the logic of justifying violence in God's name. This is *our* legacy as Christians, and we need to face it head-on, rather than trying to ignore or excuse it.

We need to take a hard look at the history of violence in God's name inspired by Scripture—not only in order to understand our religious past, but because, as long as it remains unexplored, that same ethos and logic, which has been woven into the fabric of our Western thinking, will continue to shape how we see God, how we understand justice, and how we read Scripture.

---

8   Sylvester Johnson, "New Israel, New Canaan: The Bible, the People of God, and the American Holocaust," *Union Seminary Quarterly Review* 59, no. 1–2 (2005): 25–39.

9   Cited in Jenkins, *Laying Down the Sword*, 141.

The sobering fact of history is that people have repeatedly appealed to the Bible to justify staggering acts of violence over the centuries. Again, this is not an anomaly, but an all too common part of our religious history, and the last page of that violent history has yet to be written. If we wish to reject this legacy of religiously justified bloodshed, we need to present a different way of reading the Bible which can stand against the claims of those who continue to use the Bible to justify policies of violence today, and who can marshal a host of biblical texts to support their views.

ON (NOT) DEFENDING THE BIBLE

How should we as Christians respond to violence in the Bible and what it says about the God we worship? Typically, critique of the Bible is seen as something coming from outside of the faith, while those on the inside find themselves in the position of defending and justifying Scripture.

For example, there has been a recent string of books written by the so-called "New Atheists" that focus on violence in the Bible, accusing the God found in its pages of being a moral monster. One of the central figures among the New Atheists, Richard Dawkins, writes:

The God of the Old Testament is arguably the most unpleasant character in all of fiction: jealous and proud of it; a petty, unjust, unforgiving control-freak; a vindictive, bloodthirsty ethnic cleanser; a misogynistic, homophobic, racist, infanticidal, genocidal, filicidal, pestilential, megalomaniacal, sadomasochistic, capriciously malevolent bully.[10]

Dawkins certainly does not mince words. The New Atheists typically adopt an angry and aggressive tone; and, somewhat understandably, the response of many Christian scholars and authors has been to attempt to defend and justify the violence found in the Bible, and to do so with the intent of defending the faith.

This often takes the form of either downplaying or justifying divine-sanctioned violence in some way. The 1984 *Bible Knowledge Commentary*, for example, argues that the genocide recorded in the battle of Jericho was justified so that Israel would not be "infected by the degenerate religion of the Canaanites," declaring that "pure faith and worship" could only be maintained "by the complete elimination of the Canaanites themselves."[11]

---

10 Richard Dawkins, *The God Delusion* (New York: Houghton Mifflin Harcourt, 2006), 51.

11 *Bible Knowledge Commentary: Old Testament* (Colorado Springs: David C. Cook, 1984), 342.

Adopting a similar line of reasoning, best-selling author and mega-church pastor John Ortberg writes of the Canaanite genocide:

> The beliefs of the Canaanites were a cancer that had to be removed from the land before the people of God could live there with any hope of health. Thus, God ordered surgery for the long-term health and life of his people.[12]

Foreign people are described as a "cancer" that must be eliminated for the "health" of God's people. Genocide is described and justified in cold and clinical medical terms. The chilling similarity these arguments bear to those used by the Third Reich to justify the Holocaust seems to be completely lost on these commentators.

Commenting on Psalm 137, which declares it "blessed" to smash the heads of toddlers against a rock, the recent *Two Horizons Commentary* suggests that this prayer would be more palatable to us if it we thought of it in more abstract terms:

> The modern reader ... would be much less troubled by the simple statement that it would be good when the evil Babylonian empire came to its divinely predicted end.[13]

---

12 John Ortberg, *Stepping Out in Faith: Life-Changing Examples from the History of Israel* (Grand Rapids, Zondervan, 2003), 36.

13 Geoffrey W. Grogan, *Two Horizons Old Testament Commentary: Psalms* (Grand Rapids: Eerdmans, 2008), 258.

In other words, atrocities and violence are less disturbing when its victims are thought of in impersonal and abstract terms. Try not to imagine their faces, and it isn't as upsetting. This is the advice we are given by a commentary that prides itself for its focus on the Bible's contemporary relevance and theological reflection.

It's hard to imagine anything more morally abhorrent than smashing a baby's head against a rock or committing genocide in God's name. Such actions are simply and always categorically unjustifiable—no matter what culture or time one lives in. One is hard-pressed to conceive of something more self-evident and morally obvious than this.

In fact, the *only* reason one would even think to question such an obvious claim is because of an *a priori* belief that biblical commands override conscience. When the Bible helps us challenge and deepen our moral vision and character this is surely a good thing; but when it leads us to abandon our most basic notions of morality, something has gone horribly wrong.

What makes this all the more difficult is that many of the people who say these things are caring and compassionate people. John Ortberg, for example, is well known for his commitment to care for the poor and the oppressed.

I want to emphatically stress therefore that my point is not to claim that he is a bad person because of the above comments, but just the opposite: I wish to underscore how easy it is for *all of us* as Christians—even the most loving among us—to feel the need to justify violence in the name of defending the Bible.

What causes otherwise decent and loving people like the above commentators to defend genocide in God's name? A big part of the problem has to do with the assumption that faithfulness to Scripture means accepting everything it says unquestioningly. As we can see, when applied to passages like the ones above, this unquestioning approach has often led otherwise decent people to become inadvertent advocates of appalling moral atrocities—people who normally champion compassion and moral character find themselves in the unlikely position of explaining why what appears to all of us as clear examples of abuse and atrocity are in fact good and just.

CHERRY-PICKING

While conservatives focus on explaining and justifying the violence of Scripture, moderates and progressives, on the other hand, typically attempt to focus on the positive aspects of the Bible. They commonly point out, for instance, the many verses that stress mercy and caring for the poor found in the Hebrew Scriptures. In response, both conservative Christians, as well as those like the New Atheists who are opposed to religion, will accuse them of "cherry picking" the biblical evidence.

A recent example of this can be seen in an exchange between Sojourners' president Jim Wallis and satirist and political commentator Bill Maher on HBO's *Real Time with Bill Maher*.[14] In the course of the interview, Maher—who is well known for his open criticism of religion—challenged Wallis pointedly: "How do you reconcile this idea that it all comes from the Bible, but the Bible is so flawed ... I mean, it's just so full of either nonsense or viciousness."

In response, Wallis steered the conversation back to the topic of social justice and compassion, often overlooked biblical mandates. Maher objected several times, saying, "You're not answering the question," accusing Wallis of "cherry-picking the good parts" of the Bible while ignoring the bad parts.

Contrary to how the term is sometimes (mis)used in conjunction with interpreting the Bible, it's important to understand that "cherry-picking" does not mean picking the good parts and rejecting the bad (which would generally be a very reasonable thing to do). Cherry-picking is a classic logical fallacy that involves *misrepresenting* evidence—citing only the good parts as if they are representative of the whole, while ignoring the bad parts as if they were not there.

So the issue here is not with choosing the good over the bad. Rather, it involves giving a false impression that it's all good and there is no bad. When Maher accuses Wallis of "cherry-picking the good parts" of the Bible, this is what he is referring to.

---

14   *Real Time with Bill Maher*, HBO, Episode #291 (July 26, 2013).

Now, looking at the situation in particular we can certainly appreciate why Wallis would perhaps have wanted to move the conversation away from what he likely understood as an attempt at divisiveness on Maher's part, and to instead bring the focus back to caring for the poor and immigration reform.

At the same time, the conversation about the Bible and violence is one we very much need to have as well, and it is not hard to see why critics of religion like Maher often get the impression that we moderates and progressive Christians are indeed "cooking the books," rather than honestly facing violence in Scripture.

It is therefore important that we focus on promoting these issues of compassion and social justice, while at the same time being able to put forward a biblical hermeneutic that justifies this focus which can stand its ground against conservative readings which seek to legitimize and justify violence in God's name.

Yes, there are indeed many wonderful things in the Old Testament that focus on caring for the poor, compassion, and social justice. However, as we have seen in this chapter, divine-sanctioned violence being promoted and even commanded in the Bible is not an anomaly or exception. On the contrary, it constitutes a pervasive and major theme of Scripture that simply must be faced and addressed by us if we purport to read Scripture *as* Scripture.

The liberal tendency to point to the good parts (which, indeed, are there, too) is, in and of itself, simply not a sufficient response to the truly disturbing parts that we also find in abundance in those same Scriptures. This is especially true when the implication given by such readings is that the *real* Bible is focused on mercy and hospitality, and the problem amounts to a matter of misinterpretation.

This constitutes whitewashing over the problem, rather than dealing with it. Simply ignoring the problem, or drawing attention away from it by pointing instead to the many good parts of Scripture is not the answer. When critics of religion such as Bill Maher call moderates and mainliners to the table for this, they have a legitimate point that we need to hear.

To a certain extent, we can see this "cherry-picking" tendency reflected in the common lectionaries of the Catholic and Mainline Protestant churches which, as Philip Jenkins points out in his important study of violence in the Bible, have removed nearly all the violent passages from their readings.[15] The result of this is that congregants are given the misleading impression that there is no problem of violence in the Bible.

Again, if this represents a choice as to what to emphasize and embrace, and what to reject, then this is in fact laudable.

---

15 Jenkins writes, "Absent from the lectionary, though, are other potent sections of Numbers, including the tale of Phinehas, the destruction of king Sihon, and Moses' massacre of the Midianites. The copious selections from Exodus omit sensitive passages such as the prophesy of the expulsion of the native peoples and the order to suppress Canaanite religion. While the lectionary includes the Exodus account of Moses drawing water from the rock, it cuts the very next story, that of the struggle with Amalek. Believers hear neither the warlike sections of Numbers and Deuteronomy, nor the segregationist passages of Ezra or Nehemiah. Preachers have no need to explain to their flocks such puzzling concepts as *herem*, or to discuss why Moses preserved from death only those Midianite women who remained untainted by sex." Jenkins, *Laying Down the Sword*, 205–206.

However, if there is no mention of the criteria used for evaluating what "cherries" to pick and which ones to discard, then one can easily get the false impression that there is no problem that needs to be addressed and worked through.

Jenkins thus concludes that this tendency among moderates and liberals constitutes a kind of "holy amnesia" resulting in a nearly wholesale suppression of the Bible's most aggressive passages, leaving them dangerously dormant for extremists to revive in times of conflict.

Again, at issue here is not whether we can legitimately emphasize certain parts of Scripture over others—for example, emphasizing the narrative of compassion over the narrative of vengeance. Rather, it has to do with not facing the issue of violence in Scripture *at all*, and consequently having no means with which to counter the claims of those who continue to use the Bible to justify authoritarian and state violence today.

WHAT WOULD JESUS DO?

In sum, we Christians often feel pulled between three equally unattractive options: First, there is the conservative approach of advocating things we know are profoundly wrong in an attempt to defend the Bible and our faith. The tragic results of this throughout human history are simply staggering.

Second, there is the opposite atheist approach of maintaining a conservative/fundamentalist reading, but consequently abandoning one's faith altogether in an attempt to maintain moral integrity. This is the approach of the New Atheists. The central problem here is that it fails to truly break away from the fundamentalist mindset it so despises.

Third, we have the common liberal approach of denying the problem and simply whitewashing over the evidence. As a result, while many may be attracted to the *conclusions* of this approach, they feel that it cannot be biblically sustained.

If we as progressives are going to reject violence and instead focus on mercy and social justice, then we need to have a developed hermeneutical rationale for our reading which can stand its ground against a conservative reading that seeks to legitimize violence in God's name. What we need is an approach that can honestly face and confront violence in the Bible, and do so from the perspective of faith, and as the necessary outgrowth of a developed moral conscience.

Rather than justifying or whitewashing over the problem of violence in Scripture, we instead need to confront it, and do so from the inside, as an expression of a healthy faith. There is an unfortunate tendency for people of faith—both liberal and conservative alike—to see their role in defending the faith and to perceive criticism as an outside attack to be rebutted. The prophetic spirit however is one that lovingly critiques religion from the inside, not as a way to destroy it, but as a way to make it good and whole. This was the focus of Jesus, and is characteristic

19

of how he read and applied Scripture in the context of confronting the fundamentalism of his day.

The focus of this book will therefore be on (re)discovering the radical and surprising way that Jesus read the Bible.[16] To some extent this approach may seem self-evident at first blush. After all, what Christian *wouldn't* want to read their Bible like Jesus?

However, as we will see in the next chapter, the reality is that most of us have not learned to do this at all. Despite the fact that the Gospels are filled with page after page of Jesus confronting and rebuking the religious leaders of his day for their hurtful approach to Scripture, we have somehow adopted *their* approach to biblical interpretation characterized by unquestioning obedience, rather than the approach of Jesus characterized by a hermeneutic of faithful questioning.

As it turns out, actually reading Scripture like Jesus did is in fact not common or self-evident for us at all. On the contrary, it entails an approach that scandalized the religious authorities of Jesus' time and is likely to be seen as equally subversive and "blasphemous" by the religious gatekeepers today. As subversive and surprising as Jesus' approach may be, the good news is that it holds the key to our being able to confront religious violence and abuse—both within our own faith, and within the Bible—and to do this as an act of faithfulness to God and those very Scriptures.

---

16 Many readers may be aware that because the Hebrew Scriptures had not yet at the time of Jesus been formed into the canonized collection of books Jews now know as the Tanakh and Christians as the Old Testament, it is somewhat anachronistic to refer to Jesus as reading "the Bible." The idea of our "reading the Bible like Jesus did" should therefore be understood as a colloquial shorthand for our adoption of Jesus' approach to interpreting Scripture.

With this in mind, the next chapter will take an in-depth look at the way Jesus read Scripture, in the hopes of igniting a revolution of grace in our reading as well.

CHAPTER 2

READING THE BIBLE LIKE JESUS DID

As we saw in the previous chapter, conservative Christian apologetics places its priority on defending the Bible—even when that means advocating views that we would find morally abhorrent in any other context. However, when we look at how Jesus interpreted and applied Scripture, we find that his approach was markedly different. A major source for observing the revolutionary way Jesus interpreted Scripture is his famous Sermon on the Mount. Here Jesus makes a number of statements, each beginning "you have heard that it was said" and ending "but I say to you." In each case, Jesus begins with a passage from the Old Testament and then turns the tables:

> You have heard that it was said to the people long ago, "Do not murder, and anyone who murders will be subject to judgment." But I tell you that anyone who is angry with his brother will be subject to judgment. (Matt 5:21–22)

> You have heard that it was said, "Eye for eye, and tooth for tooth." But I tell you, Do not resist an evil person. (v. 38–39)

> You have heard that it was said, "Love your neighbor and hate your enemy." But I tell you: Love your enemies and pray for those who persecute you. (v. 43–44)

Jesus prefaces these above statements by declaring, "Do not think that I have come to abolish the Law or the Prophets; I have not come to abolish them but to fulfill them" (Matt 5:17). This is often taken to mean that Jesus is in complete agreement with the law, ignoring the rather obvious fact that the very next thing Jesus does after saying this is to proceed to blatantly contradict and overturn multiple Old Testament passages and principles in the rest of his sermon.

What we need to ask ourselves is why would Jesus feel the need to stress that his intent was not to abolish the law, unless perhaps this was *exactly* what he was being accused of doing by the Pharisees and keepers of the law that he so frequently came in conflict with. Considering the reputation Jesus had among the religious leaders as a blasphemer and lawbreaker, it sure *looked to them* like he was abolishing the law. But Jesus insists that he is not coming to destroy the law, but to "fulfill" it. So what does Jesus mean by this in the context of his many following statements where he directly contradicts the law?

The Greek word translated here as "fulfill" can mean both fulfilling in the sense of meeting all the law's requirements, and it can also mean fulfillment in the sense of perfecting or completing something. Looking at what Jesus then immediately proceeds to say next after this statement, it becomes abundantly clear that he is referring to this latter sense of *perfecting* the law, lovingly bringing it into its fully intended purpose.

Let's look at this in a bit more detail: In broad strokes, Jesus is outlining a way that is rooted in forgiveness and enemy love, and is in direct opposition to the way of violent retaliation and payback justice characteristic of much of the law of Moses. Jesus contrasts the way of an "eye for an eye" for example with his new command to "not resist an evil person" (Matt 5:38–39).

Now, the way of enemy love is a complex subject that brings up many difficult questions. We will be discussing the practical application of this way in detail in a later chapter. For now however it is enough to understand that Jesus is presenting a way which he is framing as the *direct opposite* of the way of an "eye for an eye."

Now, as many have pointed out, the Mosaic legislation calling for "an eye for an eye" itself acted to curb the escalation of retributive violence, limiting it to just *one* eye for an eye instead of the 7 for Cain (Gen 4:15), and then the 77 of Lamech (Gen 4:24). In this sense, Jesus can be seen as fulfilling the intent of the Mosaic legislation to curb violence. He takes the command of an "eye for an eye" which already limited retaliation, and now takes it to the next level, saying not to retaliate *at all*, instead proposing a superior way which seeks to restore enemies, rather than to destroy them.

So while it is true that he is thus fulfilling the law in the sense of bringing it to its ultimate goal, the way he is doing this is by overturning the very system of retributive justice embodied in the law, and replacing it with the superior way of God's restorative justice rooted in the enemy love that Jesus came to demonstrate with his teaching and life. The goal is the same, but the way is radically changed, and Jesus is deliberately framing this as a radical change: "You have heard... but I say..."

Similarly, while it is frequently noted that there is no specific Old Testament command to "hate your enemy," one finds this ethos of hatred expressed frequently in the psalmist's prayers for violent vengeance against his enemies (see for example Ps 139:21-24, Ps 55:15, Ps 69:27-28, Ps 109:9-12). The policy of enemy-hate is likewise certainly epitomized in the genocide narratives, which had become a major part of the Israelites' history and identity, shaping their messianic expectations which

26

looked for a warrior messiah to come liberate them from their exile and oppression through bloodshed.

So when Jesus declared, "You have heard that it was said, 'Love your neighbor and hate your enemy,' " his audience was certainly familiar with this. As with the command to take an "eye for an eye," this deeply rooted ethos of enemy-hate in God's name is likewise overturned by Jesus. Yet Jesus does not regard any of this as abolishing the law, but as *fulfilling* it. He fulfills the law; and yet in order to do so, utterly changes it. That is how Jesus understands faithfulness to Scripture. Fulfilling Scripture for Jesus means lovingly bringing it into its fully intended purpose.

JESUS AND THE PHARISEES

The priority of Jesus was not on defending a text, it was on defending *people*—in particular defending the victims of religious violence and abuse. Jesus did this even though it meant coming into direct conflict with the religious leaders of his day and their interpretation of Scripture. We see this played out in the Gospels which record Jesus' frequent conflicts with the Pharisees and keepers of the law. What we have here is essentially a record of a conflict between two opposing ways of interpreting Scripture.

Throughout the Gospels Jesus is frequently accused by the religious authorities of breaking the law—and indeed, by their standards, he does break it. He breaks the Sabbath regulations to

27

heal (Luke 6:7–11); touches the unclean, thus making himself unclean (compare Mark 5:25–43 with Lev 15:19); and practices table fellowship with sinners (Mark 2:15; Matt 9:10; Luke 5:29; Luke 15:2). Because of all this, he is accused of being a drunk, a blasphemer, a "friend of sinners," and even in league with the devil (Luke 5:21; 7:34; 11:15). In terms of commands involving violence, John tells how Jesus refuses to participate in the execution of a woman caught in adultery as the law commanded, and instead forgives her (John 8:1–11).

What is important to recognize here is that there is no precedent for doing this allowed for in the law: While forgiveness was possible for minor trespasses through the sacrificial system, this was simply not an option for adultery. The law had given her a death sentence (Deut 22:22, Lev 20:10); but Jesus opts not to follow that law, forgiving and restoring her instead.

The overall picture that emerges here is that Jesus is presented in the Gospels as someone who continually shocked and scandalized the keepers of the law, frequently coming into open confrontation with them. On one occasion Jesus has a man with a shriveled hand stand up in front of everyone in the synagogue, and then asks, "Which is lawful on the Sabbath: to do good or to do evil, to save life or to destroy it?" (Luke 6:9).

Jesus looks around, but no one answers him.

Finally, Jesus, clearly upset and well aware that the religious authorities were carefully watching what he would do next, tells the man to stretch out his hand and then proceeds to defiantly heal him in front of everyone (v. 10). Luke tells us that this open confrontation made the Pharisees and the teachers of the law "furious" (v. 11).

Why would Jesus do this? Why would he do things that would be seen as openly breaking commandments, infuriating the religious leaders and keepers of the law? Couldn't he have waited until the next day to heal him?

In fact, they ask him this very question: "There are six days for work. So come and be healed on those days, not on the Sabbath" (Luke 13:14). Jesus refuses to wait one more day. In fact, he asks, what better day is there to heal than the Lord's day (v. 15)? Now, of course he could have waited one day in order to avoid any confrontation. The fact is, Jesus was *deliberately* courting confrontation because he saw how the religious leaders' way of interpreting and applying Scripture was hurting people, and was publicly confronting and questioning this.

There is frankly no other theme that made Jesus quite as furious as seeing people hurt in the name of religion. This is dramatically captured in his haunting rebuke "woe unto you, teachers of the law" (Matt 23:13). Jesus is opposed to their "law-keeping" because he saw how it was hurting people, pushing them away from God. Jesus acts to restore people and refuses to be held back by legal restrictions, but they do the opposite and "shut the door of the kingdom of heaven in people's faces" (v. 13). As a result, Jesus tells them, they completely miss what really matters: acting in compassion and restorative justice (v. 23).

29

While the Pharisees and teachers of the law saw Jesus as a lawbreaker, Jesus certainly did not see any of his actions as being unfaithful to God or the Bible. On the contrary, he understood his actions as directly fulfilling God's will and kingdom. Yet in faithfully acting to restore people, the Gospel writers tell us, Jesus continually *appeared* in the eyes of the religious leaders around him to be breaking God's laws. Jesus was not particularly concerned with this, and instead was infinitely more concerned with caring for the least, even if this meant his reputation became one of a "blasphemer" and "law breaker" in the eyes of the religious authorities.

This radical stance of prioritizing love over law could be said to be the baseline of Jesus' exegetical method. It is absolutely central to how Jesus understood and interpreted Scripture.[17] The take-away here is an alternative understanding of faithfulness to the Bible, rooted in compassion, that allows room for questioning and wrestling with abusive religion. We frequently see Jesus questioning and confronting the Pharisees and teachers of the law for what he understood as a hurtful and misguided interpretation of Scripture.

This was by no means a passive and timid stance, but one that openly confronts religious corruption and abuse. The conflict we see described in the Gospels between Jesus and the religious leaders therefore comes down to one of Jesus confronting an authoritarian and hurtful way of interpreting the Bible. What we

---

17　This is the conclusion reached by William Loader, who speaks of Jesus prioritizing "people more than laws." *Jesus and the Fundamentalism of His Day* (Grand Rapids: Eerdmans, 2001), 138–146.

have here in the Gospels' frequent conflicts between Jesus and the Pharisees are two diametrically opposed ways of *interpreting* the same Scriptures coming into open conflict.

The Pharisees' understanding, as it is presented in the Gospels, is characterized by a rigid observance of laws and rituals. Jesus, in contrast, had a way of interpreting the Bible that put a priority on people over rules and rituals. The way of the Pharisees is focused on fear, and thus insists on strict adherence to all of the commands, even when these commands hurt and shut people out. The way of Jesus in contrast is instead focused on what love requires—even when doing so means breaking rules and commands.

In seeking to understand these two conflicting ways of interpreting Scripture, it's imperative to stress that the conflict between Jesus and the Pharisees is not about pitting one religion against another. Rather it is an intra-Jewish dispute between two diametrically opposed understandings of what faithfulness to the same Scriptures looks like.

As the title of William Loader's study so aptly puts it, the Pharisees and other religious leaders we encounter in the New Testament are representative of what was essentially the fundamentalism of Jesus' day.[18] So what we have then is a comparison between how Jesus read Scripture, and a fundamentalist reading of Scripture.

---

18 Loader, *Jesus and the Fundamentalism of His Day*, 138–146. Note that other Pharisees, such as Hillel, would not fit into this fundamentalist mold—perhaps in a similar way to how not all Evangelical Christians do either.

It is important to stress that by the term "fundamentalist," I am not referring to those with conservative or traditional beliefs (many of which I myself affirm), but rather to a way of approaching belief that is authoritarian, judgmental, self-righteous, and ultimately fear-based.

The result of that fear is that it often can become hurtful, caring more about rules and laws than it does about the welfare of people. One does not need to look far to find these same toxic characteristics alive and well today in our own churches. Jesus, in contrast, understood faithfulness to Scripture as embodied in acts of compassion—even when that meant that he continually appeared in the eyes of the religious leaders around him to be breaking God's laws.

The question we must consider is this: Are we in fact interpreting the Bible in the way of the Pharisees, or in the way Jesus did? In order to answer this we will need to take a deeper look at what characterizes these two opposing approaches to interpreting Scripture. Here it is helpful to think of these two approaches to Scripture in the following categories: The Pharisees are representative of the way of *unquestioning obedience*, and Jesus is representative of the way of *faithful questioning*.

While the way of *unquestioning obedience* can of course be mean-spirited, this is not its key trait. Far more central is its insistence on adhering to rules, commands, and rituals even when we see that these are harming people. We can see this exemplified when the Pharisees in the Gospel accounts block a person from being healed on the Sabbath, and we can likewise see it exemplified when Christian apologists seek to explain why genocide in God's name is perhaps not so bad, or when conservative preachers insist that we should exclude certain people—even though rejecting them in this way seems wrong and hurtful to us— because "that's what the Bible says," and so we must abide by it regardless of how we feel.

This is the way of *unquestioning obedience*. Its priority is on upholding a text, at the expense of harming people, and at the expense of love. Jesus openly questions this approach to Scripture, and instead upholds that the goal of Scripture is to lead us to love. This focus leads him to *faithfully question* hurtful interpretations of Scripture. Such questioning is not only an acceptable part of a healthy faith; it is absolutely essential to it.

The Multi-Vocal Nature
of the Hebrew Scriptures

While the approach of Jesus was certainly radical, the hermeneutic of *faithful questioning* has a long and noble heritage within Judaism as well as throughout the Hebrew Scriptures. One place we can clearly observe this is in the prophets: The book of Isaiah, for example, opens with the proclamation that God "takes no pleasure" in sacrifices,

> Stop bringing meaningless offerings! Your incense is
> detestable to me ... I cannot bear your worthless assemblies
> ... Your New Moon feasts and your appointed festivals ... I
> hate with all my being. (Isa 1:11–15)

Despite the fact that the law unequivocally commanded sacrifice, Isaiah boldly disputes this, declaring that God does not want it, and in fact *hates* their worship altogether. Isaiah continues on to prophesy that God will not hear their prayers: "When you spread out your hands in prayer, I hide my eyes from you ... I am not listening."

What is the reason that Isaiah gives for this rejection of ritual? Violence. As Isaiah puts it, "Your hands are full of blood!" (v. 15). What does God instead desire? Isaiah's prophecy continues, "Learn to do right; seek justice. Defend the oppressed. Take up the cause of the fatherless; plead the case of the widow" (1:17).

Here we see the same vision of faithfulness that Jesus embraced, where our love for God is not seen in how we worship or pray or in our religious ceremonies and rituals. Rather, it is seen in how we treat others, especially the least. The true fast, the real sacrifice that God wants, Isaiah insists, is one of showing compassion to those in need.

This is the way of *faithful questioning* motivated by compassion. It is a way of interpreting Scripture—found in both Testaments—that involves challenging the law in the interest of prioritizing compassion towards others over rigid compliance to rules. As we have seen with Jesus, if a law seemed unloving, not only did he feel free to break it, he felt an *obligation* to break it, because that is what true faithfulness to Scripture looked like in his eyes.

For Jesus, questioning religious violence in ourselves, in our faith, and in our sacred text is a moral imperative. Compassion and character compel us to question, and that questioning in the name of love is modeled for us in Scripture itself. As Old Testament scholar Terence Fretheim puts it, "An inner-biblical warrant exists for the people of God to raise questions."[19]

Contrary to popular opinion, the Old Testament is not a single book with one unified view of who God is and how life works. It is instead a collection of books from multiple authors who articulate *a multitude of opposing perspectives*.

In light of this, Old Testament scholar Walter Brueggemann describes the Hebrew Bible as consisting of what he calls *testimony and counter-testimony*. The picture here is of many witnesses in a court, each arguing their case, disputing, contradicting each other. This is, Brueggemann says, the "primary mode of articulation" in the Old Testament—one that is, by it's very nature, "disputatious and permeated with contrariness."[20] In the Hebrew Bible, we do not hear a single unified voice, rather we encounter multiple competing voices—each claiming to be the correct view, each claiming authority.

19 Terence E. Fretheim, "God and Violence in the Old Testament" *Word & World* 24.1 (2004) 18–28 at 26.

20 Walter Brueggemann, *Theology of the Old Testament: Testimony, Dispute, Advocacy* (Minneapolis: Fortress, 2005). preface to the 2005 edition.

The Old Testament is a record of dispute. This dispute can be characterized as consisting of an ongoing debate between two key narratives: On the one side is the majority narrative of *unquestioning obedience*, and on the other is the protesting minority voice of *faithful questioning*.

We can see, for example, the majority narrative of demanding unquestioning obedience in the form of violence exemplified in the Old Testament's genocide commands, and in the story of Abraham's sacrifice of Isaac. In this narrative, if God says to kill, you just do it, no questions asked. Questioning is portrayed here as a sin. King Saul, for example, loses his entire kingdom because he hesitates to commit complete genocide as God had commanded (1 Samuel 15).

Elsewhere however we encounter an opposing narrative where questioning is presented as a virtue: Over and over, we see the heroes of the Hebrew Bible disputing, lamenting, and questioning divine-sanctioned violence. This counter-narrative of faithful protest and questioning can be seen in Abraham's challenge to God, "Will not the Judge of all the earth do right?" where Abraham pleads with God not to destroy Sodom (Gen 18:25). Similarly, Moses argues with God not to act in violence against Israel (Exod 32:7–14). We see such protest throughout the Psalms and prophets as well, and of course we see it over and over again in Jesus.

It's critical to recognize the direct connection between the narrative of *unquestioning obedience* and its frequent appeal to threat and violence in God's name. This narrative is grounded in the promise of reward for those who obey and punishment for those who do not, exemplified in Deuteronomy's list of "blessings and curses" which promises success, health, and riches for those who obey the law, but plagues, poverty, and stomach-turning violent suffering for those who disobey.

Deuteronomy 28 declares that if the Israelites break the law, the Lord will inflict them with a host of physical and mental illnesses—their children will be abducted as slaves, their fiancees will be raped before their eyes—and crescendos with the gruesome declaration that even "the most tenderhearted man among you will have no compassion for his own brother, his beloved wife, and his surviving children" (v. 54) because everyone will become insane cannibals eating their own family.

That's what will happen "if you refuse to obey all the words of instruction that are written in this book, and if you do not fear the glorious and awesome name of the Lord your God" (v. 58). In this narrative, if someone is sick or the victim of violence, it was assumed that they must have sinned. If someone was rich or successful in battle, it was assumed they must be obeying God.

In contrast to this, throughout the Psalms we find a protest against this narrative where the psalmist repeatedly laments that the wicked are prospering, calling out for God to rescue him from unjust suffering. Again, there is a connection here to violence in that the narrative of *faithful questioning* exemplified here involves specifically questioning and *protesting* the violence

37

they are suffering as being unjust. The psalmist is protesting against violence, as are Abraham and Moses.

Of all of these many voices of protest against divine-sanctioned violence found within the Hebrew Bible, the most powerful is the voice of Job, who accuses God of injustice because of his suffering. "Though I cry, 'Violence!' I get no response; though I call for help, there is no justice" (Job 19:7).

While Job's friends echo Deuteronomy 28, insisting that his sickness and suffering are deserved as a punishment for his sin, Job insists on his innocence. Job's testament of *faithful questioning* stands in contrast to his friends counter-witness of *unquestioning obedience*. Perhaps the most remarkable part of the book of Job is God's answer to his friends, "I am angry with you and your two friends, because you have not spoken the truth about me, as my servant Job has" (Job 42:7).

In such places the voices of the victims are heard for the first time, allowing them to make the case for their innocence. As Rene Girard observes, this was unique in world literature where it was exceptional at the time for the voice of the victim to be heard at all.[21] Instead, history is normally told from the perspective of the victors, demonizing and dehumanizing the vanquished. In that narrative, those who suffer are evil and deserving of their suffering.

---

21 See the summary of Girard's position in René Girard, *I See Satan Fall Like Lightning* (Maryknoll: Orbis, 2001) xvii–xviii, as well as the longer discussion in *Things Hidden Since the Foundation of the World* (Stanford University Press: Stanford, 1987) 144–158.

The inclusion of this minority voice of the victim within its canon is something that sets the Hebrew Bible apart from other writings of the time, especially because it maintains, against the voice of authority, that their suffering is unjust. This is revolutionary in the sense that the inclusion of this voice of protest has the power to expose and subvert the oppression and harm of the dominant voice.

While this perspective of the innocent victim is deeply significant, it is important to note that the Psalms and Job nevertheless continue to reflect the ethos of the law which declared that the just would prosper and the wicked would suffer. They do not themselves question the justice of this system, but instead complain that it was not being upheld. The psalmist does not regard himself in Paul's terms as a sinner in need of mercy, but instead as blameless and righteous.

The Psalms therefore do not propose mercy and love for enemies, but call for God's wrath. So in the protests of the penitential Psalms and Job, while we find something deeply significant, we are not yet at the place of forgiveness and enemy love. What we however can see in the Psalms is the voice of the victim emerging out of the crowd, given voice for the first time. These are the ones that formerly were scapegoated, condemned, dehumanized, but who Jesus saw and loved. This is the cry of *the least of these*.

This all illustrates the fact that rather than finding a single narrative throughout the Old Testament, we instead repeatedly encounter these conflicting perspectives within the Hebrew canon: One narrative states that suffering and violence are just and deserved, the other protests and argues against that narrative, calling it unjust.

These competing narratives zig-zag back and forth throughout the Old Testament, cataloging an ongoing dispute. While the Psalms and Job confront and challenge the narrative of reward and punishment found in Deuteronomy 28, the prophets pick up on this theme again, announcing that the reason the Israelites are suffering famine, slavery, rape, and sickness is because they have sinned. If they will only repent, the prophets claim, all this would stop.

Jesus, while embracing the prophets' priority of compassion over ritual, rejects their common tactic of blaming the victim, and instead acts to heal those who are sick, effectively undoing God's supposed "judgment" on them. Jesus, in fact, does not associate sickness with God's judgment at all, but with the kingdom of Satan, and thus acts to liberate people from its bondage, rather than upholding it as right and calling for repentance as the prophets do. Jesus therefore rejects the prophets' claim that such judgment (sickness, suffering, etc.) is God's work, and instead frames his healing ministry in terms of the kingdom of God advancing against Satan's kingdom (cf. Luke 11:17–20).

A notable exception to the prophets' characteristic tactic of blaming the victim as a way of explaining suffering is the theme of the Suffering Servant in Isaiah. Here, similar to Job, the view instead is that the servant was blameless, and his suffering was a picture of oppression and injustice,

> He was oppressed, and he was afflicted, yet he did not open his mouth; like a lamb that is led to the slaughter...
> By a perversion of justice he was taken away.
> (Isa 53:7-8, NRSV)

The image of the Suffering Servant—including the larger theme of suffering for righteousness which Jesus declares "Blessed"—is of course one that Jesus clearly does identify with.

We can see from all of this that Jesus embraced some parts of Scripture as being applicable to and descriptive of his messianic mission and ministry, as well as reflecting God's kingdom and way, while other parts he either ignores, reinterprets, or—as we have seen in his "but I say to you" statements— even directly contradicts.

An important example of this can be seen in how Jesus at the last supper reinterprets the Passover in light of his own impending passion. Here Christ links his impending death and resurrection to the central defining story of Judaism, the Exodus. At the same time, there are significant differences: Jesus identifies with the story of a people's liberation from bondage, but does not identify with the genocide narrative that follows this as the people entered the promised land and mass slaughtered the local inhabitants.

41

Even within the story of the Passover itself, there are many significant differences. The ransom of the Passover was accomplished through a demonstration of violent force, and many people at the time expected the messiah to "save" through violent force as well. This however was clearly not how Jesus understood his messianic mission. Likewise, while the enemies in Passover were other people, the "enemy" in the gospel is evil itself, and all of humanity are the recipients of God's deliverance.

Jesus embraces the story of the exodus, but applies it in a way that is different, unexpected, and transforming. Christ's death is thus analogous to Passover, while at the same time it is utterly different from it. Stop and let that sink in for a moment: Because of the multi-vocal quality of the Old Testament, we see Jesus embracing certain narratives that speak of restoration and mercy, and rejecting other narratives found in those same Scriptures which instead uphold committing or justifying violence in God's name.

Not only does Jesus reject these narratives, he attributes them to the way of the devil, rather than the way of God. Consider for example the story of Elijah calling down fire from heaven as proof that he was on God's side. Elijah declares, "If I am a man of God, may fire come down from heaven and consume you and your fifty men!" Then fire fell from heaven and consumed the captain and his men (2 Kings 1:10). Hoping to follow Elijah's example, James and John ask Jesus in response to opposition they were experiencing, "Lord, do you want us to call fire down from heaven to destroy them?" (Luke 9:54–55). Perhaps that was why they got their nickname "the sons of thunder."

Luke tells us that the response of Jesus was not to affirm this narrative, but to sternly rebuke his disciples. In that rebuke of Jesus is an implicit yet clear rejection of the way of Elijah as well. Later manuscripts include the response of Jesus, "You do not know what kind of spirit you are of, for the Son of Man did not come to destroy men's lives, but to save them" (Luke 9:55–56).[22] In other words, Jesus is essentially saying that the way of Elijah is not of God, but instead belongs to the spirit of the one who seeks to destroy, that is, of the devil.

While Elijah claimed that his actions proved he was a "man of God," this passage in Luke's Gospel makes the opposite claim: The true "man of God" incarnate had not come to obliterate life, but to save, heal, and restore it (Luke 19:10 & John 3:17). Jesus not only recognizes this himself as the Son of God, but rebukes James and John for not having come to this conclusion on their own. In other words, Jesus *expects* his disciples—expects you and me—to be making these same calls of knowing what to embrace in the Bible and what to reject.

The Old Testament is a record of dispute which makes room for questions by its very nature. Because of this, it calls us to enter into that dispute ourselves as we read. In fact, because of its multiple conflicting narratives we simply must choose, we *must*

---

22 Even if this verse is a later addition representing a sort of biblical commentary by the early church, it certainly reflects the ethos of Jesus as well, who consistently rejected violent force as a vehicle of the Kingdom (see for example Matt 26:52–54 and John 18:36).

take sides in the debate, we are forced to embrace some narratives, while rejecting others.

The key difference between Jesus and the Pharisees described in the Gospel accounts is in *which narratives they chose to embrace.* Similarly, the question for us is not *whether or not* we will choose, but rather *which* narratives we choose to embrace, and *how* will we choose them? This book's central proposal is that we as followers of Jesus need to learn to adopt the same priorities that Jesus did in his interpretation of Scripture.

LEARNING TO QUESTION

It's commonly asserted that Jesus affirmed the Old Testament simply by virtue of the fact that he quoted from it. As we've seen however, this claim simply does not hold up to scrutiny. The Gospels' frequent accounts of Jesus' confrontations with the Pharisees demonstrate that Jesus made a habit of questioning and rejecting how Scripture was read and applied whenever he saw that this was hurting people. This led Jesus to embrace some parts of Scripture which focused on compassion.

When Jesus saw that the Pharisees were instead embracing parts of Scripture which justified doing the opposite, he opposed them. Such acts of *faithful questioning* were how Jesus understood faithfulness to Scripture because Jesus understood that the aim of

Scripture was to love. A reading that leads to harm rather than love is therefore a wrong reading. Jesus' way of *faithful questioning* stands in sharp contrast to the Pharisees' stance of *unquestioning obedience*, and the core reason that Jesus rejected this way is because he saw that the way of *unquestioning obedience* harms people. It still does today.

A faithful reading of Scripture is therefore not about defending the bad parts of the Bible (whether by seeking to justify or downplay them). On the contrary, a faithful reading entails wrestling with those troubling texts as the biblical authors did themselves. Because the Old Testament is a record of dispute, it calls us by its very nature to enter into that dispute ourselves as we read. In fact, because of its multiple conflicting narratives we simply have no choice but to choose; we *must* take sides in the debate; we are forced to embrace some narratives while rejecting others. As Brueggemann writes:

> Countertestimony is not an act of unfaith. It is rather a characteristic way in which faith is practiced. Israel's faith is a probing, questioning, insisting, disjunctive faith.[23]

To be sure, the narrative of compassion and questioning is a minority voice in the Old Testament. One might even rightly argue that *unquestioning obedience* represents the majority narrative of the Old Testament. The way of reading the Bible we see in Jesus and the prophets—characterized by *faithful questioning*—has

---

23 Brueggemann, *Theology of the Old Testament* , 318.

always been a minority voice, both within Judaism and Christianity.

The counter-narrative of questioning and caring for victims is a dissident voice, a voice from the margins. It is the voice of the prophet calling out in the wilderness. It is the voice of the one who was rejected and crucified by the religious and political authorities.

While the way of *faithful questioning* is a voice from the margins, this is precisely where we find Jesus. The narrative Jesus prioritized when he read his Bible was not the majority narrative of power and violence, but the minority voice of questioning in the name of compassion. If we wish to read our Bibles like Jesus, then we will need to learn to hear the minority voices, and adopt his way of reading from the margins.

Learning to read Scripture from the margins like Jesus did is of course no easy task. For many of us this will involve re-thinking our entire approach to exegesis and relationship with Scripture. Rest assured that we will spend a lot of time working out the details of what this looks like practically in our faith and life as the book progresses. However, every journey begins with a first step, and the place to start here is by recognizing that when we are asking hard questions about disturbing passages in the Bible we find ourselves in the company of the many counter-voices within the Bible who are doing the same. When we do this, we are engaging the Bible in the same way the prophets did, and the same way Jesus did. That's a very good place to be.

CHAPTER 3

PAUL'S CONVERSION FROM VIOLENCE

As we've seen, Jesus came into sharp conflict with the Pharisees and the hurtful way they read the Bible. The book of Acts tells us of one Pharisee in particular named Saul who was active in violently persecuting the early church, including participating in the lynching of Stephen (Acts 7:54–58). As you probably know, that young Pharisee ended up converting to Christ. We know him today as the Apostle Paul. A question that is seldom asked, however, is what would have led a zealous Pharisee like Paul to reject the violent understanding of religion that he had formerly embraced? Further, how did he come to view the Scriptures that he had formerly marshaled to justify violence in God's name?

We can catch a glimpse of this in Paul's later critique of the law. The law itself, he says, is not the medium of salvation, but is "powerless" to save (Rom 8:3). Paul provocatively tells his readers that they are "not under law, but under grace" (Rom 6:14) and declares that while the Spirit gives life, the "letter kills" (2 Cor 3:6). It would be hard to overstate how radical and shocking these declarations must have sounded to his fellow Jews.

What is it that drove Paul to make such scandalous statements about the law? Paul becomes absolutely livid when he finds the Galatians are returning to "the works of the law," declaring that way was *anathema* or "damned to hell" (Gal 1:9), and emphatically states that "if righteousness could be gained through the law, Christ died for nothing!" (Gal 2:21). What is going on here that has Paul so worked up? What made Paul come to consider his former religious education and Bible training, as well as his status and credentials as a "Hebrew of Hebrews," all to be "garbage" (Phil 3:8)? What led him to the conviction that anyone who follows that way was "under a curse" (Gal 3:10)?

I want to suggest that the reason for Paul's repulsion lies in his own past history of religious violence. Paul had seen firsthand where this all led. He knew from experience the damage and harm caused by his violent religious past.

Recent scholarship, known as "the New Perspective on Paul," has helpfully drawn attention to the fact that Paul's critique of the law is not about opposing so-called "good works" (i.e., acts of love and mercy) as the typical Lutheran interpretation of Paul had said. Rather, like Jesus, Paul saw fulfillment of the law as embodied in compassion, rather than in legal ritualistic observance.[24] In other words, Paul's problem was not with the law itself, which he understood as having the ultimate goal of leading to love, but with a particular hurtful way of interpreting and applying the law (and thus Scripture) that prioritized rituals and rules over love (cf. Rom 13:8–10).

Luther's struggle was with keeping a strict moral code, and his feeling of guilt at his failings. What the New Perspective on Paul helpfully points out is that, as important as this may have been for Luther and for many others like him, this was not in fact Paul's struggle.

Remember, Paul's conversion to Christ was not one of a "sinner" who finds religion. Paul already had religion, and describes himself in fact as a religious zealot who could boast that his observance of the Torah was "faultless" (Phil 3:6). So while Luther might say "no one can keep the law," Paul here declares that he had in fact kept it flawlessly.

---

24 Loader's analysis of Jesus and the law closely parallels the (new) perspective of Paul, which also sees fulfillment of the law as embodied in compassion rather than in legal ritualistic observance. See James D. G. Dunn, *Jesus, Paul and the Law: Studies in Mark and Galatians* (Louisville: Westminster/John Knox, 1990).

Yet despite this, Paul came to regard himself as "the worst of all sinners" and "a violent man" (1 Tim 1:13, 15). He confesses painfully, "I do not even deserve to be called an apostle, because I persecuted the church of God" (1 Cor 15:9). Paul's own self-described sin was one that was committed in the name of religion. It was not a sin that came from a failure to keep the law, but one committed in the practice of carrying it out and defending it by means of violence.

Paul's conversion was one *away from religious fanaticism*. In other words, Paul did not see himself as rejecting his Jewish faith or Israel's scriptures, but rather as rejecting his former violent interpretation of them. Paul's great sin—as he came to understand it—had been *participation in what he understood as religiously justified acts of violence, motivated by religious zeal*.

Paul's sin was the sin of religious violence, and this is the reason Paul was so adamantly opposed to forms of religion, as well as interpretations of Scripture, that he recognized as promoting violence in God's name. This is the motivation at the heart of Paul's critique of the law.

For this reason Pauline scholar James Dunn describes Paul's conversion as a conversion away from religion characterized by "zealous and violent hostility."[25] Paul connects his zeal to religious violence directly when he writes "as for zeal, persecuting the church" (Phil 3:6). Paul's term "zeal" is worth exploring in a bit more detail. As NT Wright puts it:

---

25 Dunn, *Theology of Paul the Apostle* (Grand Rapids: Eerdmans, 1998), 353.

For the first century Jew, zeal was something you did with a knife. Those first-century Jews who longed for revolution against Rome looked back to Phinehas and Elijah in the Old Testament, and to the Maccebean heroes two centuries before Paul, as their models. They saw themselves as being "zealous for YHWH," "zealous for Torah," and as having the right, and the duty, to put that zeal into operation with the use of violence.[26]

Similarly, Dunn describes this "zeal" as "an unconditional commitment to maintain Israel's distinctiveness, to prevent the purity of its covenant set-apartness to God from being adulterated or defiled ... expressed precisely in the slaughter of those who threatened Israel's distinctive covenant status ... *[T]his must be what Paul had in mind when he speaks of himself as a 'zealot' and of his 'zeal' manifested in persecution of the church.*"[27]

Here in this language of "purity" and the use of violence to prevent Israel from being "adulterated or defiled," we can see clear echoes of the genocide command of 1 Samuel 15 mentioned in chapter one (as well as the Bible commentators' own rationalizations who likewise describe the mass slaughter of men, women, and infant children as "a cancer that had to be removed"). That same logic of using divine-sanctioned violence to preserve purity had driven Paul to violently persecute the church. So while we have seen that Jesus rejected the violent way

---

26 NT Wright, *What Saint Paul Really Said* (Grand Rapids: Eerdmans, 1997) 27.

27 Dunn, *Theology of Paul the Apostle*, 351. See also Michael Gorman *Inhabiting the Cruciform God* (Grand Rapids: Eerdmans, 2009) 131–142. Emphasis added.

of Elijah; Paul in contrast had formerly seen Elijah's example of violence as an inspiration and model.

In sum, before his conversion, Paul had read his Bible and concluded that he should commit violence in God's name. After his encounter with Christ, and his experience of healing and enemy love from Jesus' disciples (Acts 9:11–18), Paul needed to completely reassess how to understand the Scripture he had previously read in this toxic and violent way, leading him to a radically different understanding of God's will, and a radically different way of interpreting those same Scriptures.

DELETING VIOLENCE FROM THE BIBLE

We now turn to explore in more detail just how Paul's reading of Scripture radically changed after his conversion away from religious violence, with a particular focus on how Paul deals with violent passages in the Old Testament that call for killing Gentiles.

In Romans 15, for example, Paul quotes several scriptural passages to illustrate how Gentiles "may glorify God for his mercy" because of the gospel (verse 9). Highly significant is what Paul omits from these passages:

> For I tell you that Christ has become a servant of the Jews on behalf of God's truth, to confirm the promises made to the patriarchs so that the Gentiles may glorify God for his mercy, as it is written: "~~I destroyed my foes. They cried for help, but there was no one to save them—to the LORD, but he did not answer ... He is the God who avenges me, who puts the Gentiles under me~~... Therefore I will praise you among the Gentiles; I will sing hymns to your name." [quoting Psalm 18:41–49]

> Again, it says, "Rejoice, O Gentiles, with his people, ~~for he will avenge the blood of his servants; he will take vengeance on his enemies and make atonement for his land and people.~~" [Deut 32:43]

Paul has removed the references to violence against Gentiles, and re-contextualized these passages to instead declare God's mercy in Christ for Gentiles. This constitutes a major redefinition of how salvation is conceived: Instead of salvation meaning God "delivering" the ancient Israelites from the hands of their enemies through military victory (as described in Psalm 18, which Paul is quoting from), Paul now understands salvation to mean the restoration of all people in Christ, including those same "enemy" Gentiles.

Paul's focus in Romans was on the inclusion of Gentiles into the promise of Israel. This is the polar opposite of what his focus had formerly been when he had instead embraced the narrative of violent zeal and purity. Surely Paul had formerly read these passages, which clearly speak of the slaughter of Gentiles, and used them to justify violence in God's name. So it is no coincidence that he now picks these same passages to declare God's love and grace towards Gentiles with his radical editing of these texts.

There are plenty of other passages in the Old Testament that speak of showing mercy to Gentiles, of welcoming them in. These speak of Israel being a "light to the Gentiles" (Isa 49:6) by being an example of love and good. We can see that the Gospel writers connected this narrative with Jesus (see for example Isaiah 42 cited in Matt 12:18–21 and Luke 4:18). Paul could have easily quoted any of these to make his case. Instead, he quotes the very passages that speak of bloody vengeance and slaughter of Gentiles. Is Paul deliberately subverting these passages— converting them away from violence, just as he had been converted by Christ?

Remarking on the way Paul quotes these passages with a complete disregard to authorial intent, New Testament scholar Richard Hays once joked that Paul would have surely flunked a seminary class in exegesis. But, as Hays himself argues, Paul was in fact intimately familiar with the original context of these passages, as were his readers. Given this, it seems rather implausible to regard this simply as a case of sloppy exegesis. A more likely conclusion is that Paul is deliberately reversing the meaning—turning the tables in order to provoke his audience.

This is especially evident in Romans 3:10-18, where Paul paints a picture of human fallenness, weaving together several passages from the Psalms and prophets:

As it is written,
"There is no one righteous, not even one; there is no one who understands, no one who seeks God. All have turned away, they have together become worthless; there is no one who does good, not even one." [quoting Psalm 14:1–3]

"Their throats are open graves; their tongues practice deceit." [Psalm 5:9]

"The poison of vipers is on their lips." [Psalm 140:3]

"Their mouths are full of cursing and bitterness."
[Psalm 10:7]

"Their feet are swift to shed blood; ruin and misery mark their ways, and the way of peace they do not know."
[Isaiah 59:7–8]

"There is no fear of God before their eyes." [Psalm 36:1]

Note that Paul's list of sins is focused on acts of hatred and violence: deceit and poisonous words, cursing and bitterness, killing, misery, and the behavior of those who don't know "the way of peace." Read in their original context, these first three psalms each make a clear distinction between outside "evildoers" and the "righteous" in-group. For example, in the verse immediately following Paul's first quotation, Psalm 14 continues, "Will evildoers never learn—those who devour my people as men eat bread and who do not call on the Lord? There they are, overwhelmed with dread, for God is present in the company of the righteous."

To fully appreciate what Paul is doing here it is important to recall the structure of Paul's argument in Romans 1–3: Paul begins in the first chapter of Romans by painting a picture of pagan cultic worship that would have been seen as appalling to his audience.

One can imagine them fervently nodding in approval when Paul says that God's wrath is coming because of this, thinking, "Those hated Gentile outsiders are finally going to get what they have coming!"

But then Paul suddenly turns the tables on his religious audience in chapter two, declaring "You, therefore, have no excuse, you who pass judgment on someone else" (Rom 2:1), challenging his audience's tendency towards self-righteous judgmentalism, and pointing out their own hypocrisy. They have no room to judge because they are just as guilty, Paul says.

Ever since Luther, it has been common to read Romans from the perspective of one asking how they can escape God's wrath; but recent scholarship has drawn attention to the fact that this was not at all Paul's focus. Instead, Paul is addressing a religious audience who longed for God to come in wrath and punish sinners. In other words, Paul is addressing people who see things the way he used to.

In Romans 3:25, Paul says that God chose the shocking vehicle of the cross in order to "demonstrate his righteousness, because in his forbearance he had left the sins committed beforehand unpunished." The New Living Translation puts it like this: "This sacrifice shows that God was being fair when he held back and did not punish those who sinned in times past."

Paul stresses this because, in the eyes of his Jewish audience, God's *not* judging and punishing sin was seen as unjust. As a people long in exile, living under pagan oppression, they wanted God to come in wrath and judge the Gentile sinners. God judging sin meant for them that the victims would be avenged. So when God did not come in wrath as they had hoped, this seemed in their eyes to be unjust.

Similarly, the psalms that Paul is quoting from here are all written from the perspective of the "righteous" one longing to see the "wicked" be destroyed, echoing the perspective Paul formerly held, and echoing the perspective of Paul's audience in Romans. The very next psalm Paul quotes specifically calls out for judgment— "Declare them guilty, O God! Let their intrigues be their downfall" (Psalm 5:10)—and again contrasts "the wicked" (v. 4) with "the righteous" whom God favors: "For surely, O Lord, you bless the righteous; you surround them with your favor as with a shield" (v. 12).

Paul is making a very different point here from the original intent of these psalms. In fact, he is making the *opposite* point: We should not cry out for God's wrath and judgment, because we are all sinners in need of mercy. Not only is Paul attempting to convert his audience away from religious violence and to the way of God's restorative justice revealed in Jesus, Paul is doing the same with his Bible.

Paul's conclusion here demonstrates his awareness that he has radically changed the meaning of these passages: "Now we know that whatever the law says, it says to those who are under the law, so that every mouth may be silenced and the whole world held accountable to God" (Rom 3:19). In effect, Paul says: Now we know of course that this was originally said of Gentile outsiders —but really what the law says, it says to those of us on the inside. So these verses are in fact speaking to us; we are no better.

This is not a case of careless, out-of-context proof-texting. Paul has artfully and deliberately reshaped these psalms from their original cry for divine violence into a confession of universal culpability, highlighting that all of us need mercy.

This same pattern can be found throughout Paul's letters. Paul is not simply finding references to Christ Jesus in Jewish Scripture. He finds radical new meaning in these texts to show the way of Jesus, the way of overcoming evil with good, the gospel of grace. Just as Jesus had not come to condemn but to redeem humanity, this transformative hermeneutic ultimately seeks to redeem these passages rather than reject them—to

58

"fulfill" rather than to destroy. They are "converted" as we are. Thus we might speak of this New Testament hermeneutic as *redemptive transformation* resulting in the *disarmament* of these texts.

A wonderful example of this is found in Paul's Easter message in 1 Cor 15 where he writes that "The last enemy to be destroyed is death" (1 Cor 15:26). Paul then quotes the familiar line "Where, O death, is your victory? Where, O death, is your sting?" and declares that "The sting of death is sin, and the power of sin is the law. But thanks be to God! He gives us the victory through our Lord Jesus Christ" (1 Cor 15:55-57). As Paul is using it, the phrase, "Where, O death, is your victory? Where, O death, is your sting?" is addressing a defeated death: "Where is your sting now, O death? For you have been defeated by Christ!" But take a look at the original passage in Hosea that Paul is quoting from:

> Shall I ransom them from the power of Sheol? Shall I redeem them from Death?
>
> O Death, where are your plagues? O Sheol, where is your destruction?
>
> Compassion is hidden from my eyes. (Hos 13:14 NRSV)

The sense here is the *opposite* of what Paul is saying. It is about *inviting* death to come and destroy Israel in punishment. The New English Translation makes this difference quite clear:

59

Will I deliver them from the power of Sheol? No, I will not!
Will I redeem them from death? No, I will not!

O Death, bring on your plagues! O Sheol, bring on your
destruction!

My eyes will not show any compassion! (Hos 13:14 NET)

Hosea is not mocking death, but calling for death. How do we
know that this is what Hosea meant? *Context.* Look at the last line:
"Compassion is hidden from my eyes." When we read a few
verses further we see that the chapter concludes by declaring,

They will fall by the sword; their little ones will be dashed to
the ground, their pregnant women ripped open. (Hos 13:16
NIV)

This was not good news when Hosea said it, but Paul has
turned it around. He has taken a passage which in its original
context was about violence and death being poured out on
people, and transformed it into a declaration of how humanity
has been liberated from death because of the Resurrection where
Christ overcame and defeated death. Paul is reversing the
original context, subverting it, redeeming it.

Paul's story is instructive because it is a story of a conversion
—not a conversion from one religion to another, but a conversion
away from a toxic form of zealous fundamentalism found in all

60

forms of religion that sanctify and glorify violence in God's name. The reading that justified violence in God's name which Paul now rejects is precisely the one he had formerly embraced as a Pharisee.

Paul's realization was that his own religious zeal had tragically led him to become "a violent man" in God's name, and as a result "the worst of sinners" (1 Tim 1:13, 15). In other words, Paul had read the Bible extensively, religiously, zealously, *and had gotten God completely wrong*. It wasn't until he was encountered by Jesus that he was able to go back and re-read Scripture in the light of Christ, consequently embracing a radically different narrative of grace and enemy love found in those same pages.

PROCLAIMING GRACE NOT WRATH

We can get an idea of how provocative Paul's editing and disarming of Scripture would have seemed to his audience at the time by comparing it to a similar instance where Jesus employed this same method when he read from Isaiah in the synagogue at the inauguration of his ministry:

The Spirit of the Lord is on me, because he has anointed me to preach good news to the poor. He has sent me to proclaim freedom for the prisoners and recovery of sight for the blind, to release the oppressed, to proclaim the year of

61

the Lord's favor ~~and the day of vengeance of our God~~ (Luke 4:18–19)

Jesus stops reading here mid-sentence, omitting the ending which announces "the day of vengeance of our God" (Isa 61:2). This would have been something that the people had been looking forward to, hoping for. The awaited time when the Roman oppressors would have finally gotten theirs!

Luke tells us that after cutting this sentence in half, Jesus "rolled up the scroll, gave it back to the attendant and sat down" (v. 20). Then, with everyone's eyes fixed on him, Jesus announces, "Today this scripture is fulfilled in your hearing" (v. 20–21). In other words, the part about preaching good news to the poor, sight for the blind, and release of the captives is fulfilled in Jesus, but *not* the part about God's vengeance. That part isn't going to happen. Luke then describes the reaction of the people, which sounds very positive:

> All spoke well of him and were amazed at the gracious words that came from his lips. "Isn't this Joseph's son?" they asked. (Luke 4:22)

Most translations render this as the New International Version (NIV) does above, "All *spoke well of him (emartyroun autō)* and *were amazed (ethaumazon)*." Both of these verbs however are ambiguous in the Greek. *Martyreō* with the dative can mean both "testify for" or "testify against," and *thaumazō* can mean "to wonder" either in the sense of enthusiasm, or of shock.[28] So this verse can equally be translated as follows:

> All *bore witness against him* (*emartyroun autō*) and *were shocked* (*ethaymazon*) at the words of grace coming from his mouth. "Isn't this Joseph's son!?" they asked. (Luke 4:22)

A major indicator as to which of these possible readings we should adopt can be found in what happens next: Jesus' response to their exclamation is to answer with an angry rebuke, declaring "no prophet is accepted in his hometown!" (v. 24). This indicates that their question "Isn't this Joseph's son?" was not a compliment, as if to say "Wow, that's wonderful, Joseph must be so proud!" but rather something more akin to "Can anything good come out of Nazareth?" (John 1:46). Jesus' rebuke continues:

> I assure you that there were many widows in Israel in Elijah's time, when the sky was shut for three and a half years and there was a severe famine throughout the land. Yet Elijah was not sent to any of them, but to a widow in Zarephath in the region of Sidon. And there were many in Israel with leprosy in the time of Elisha the prophet, yet not one of them was cleansed—only Naaman the Syrian." (Luke 4:25–27)

---

28 I. Howard Marshall, *The Gospel of Luke: A Commentary on the Greek Text* (Grand Rapids: Eerdmans, 1978) 186. Joachim Jeremias, *New Testament Theology* (New York: Charles Scribner & Sons, 1971) 206–7.

Both the widow in Zarephath and Naaman the Syrian in are Gentiles. Jesus is stating that while there were many in Israel who were hungry and sick, *Gentiles* were the recipients of God's providence and healing here. In other words, in case his audience had not gotten why he left out the part from Isaiah about vengeance towards Gentiles, now with these two passages Jesus spells it out for them.

Luke tells us that the people "were furious" and "drove him out of the town ... in order to throw him down the cliff" (Luke 4:28–29). Based on this extreme reaction—one where they want to kill him—it's hard to believe that they were complimenting him just moments before, and much more likely that the people's initial reaction was one of shock and condemnation at Jesus' message of grace *without* wrath. Everyone likes hearing a message of grace toward ourselves, but we don't so much like hearing a message of grace for our enemies.

Just as Paul's religious audience in Romans was longing for wrath, so too was the audience of Jesus here. They believed—like so many still do today—that the way justice is fulfilled is by the destruction of their enemies. Jesus and Paul are both confronting this common religious belief that God's justice comes about through the violent destruction of the "bad people."

This violent view was at the heart of the common Jewish messianic expectation which hoped for God to come in vengeance, and thus understood the messiah as a warrior king who would vanquish the pagan oppressors and restore Israel to its glory. As we can see in this passage, the people are thus pleased when they hear that Jesus will work to liberate the people from their oppression. However, when they understand that this will involve showing grace and not vengeance to Gentiles, they become furious with Jesus and try to kill him.

As we have seen from looking at the fuller context of Paul's scriptural quotations (in particular the violent parts Paul excluded), this particular messianic expectation is supported by many passages in the Old Testament prophets. It should be abundantly clear, however, that this was not at all how Jesus understood his messianic mission, nor how Paul proclaimed the message of God's grace to those Gentiles.

THE COMMON DENOMINATOR OF LOVE

Generally speaking, Paul and Jesus had different rhetorical and literary styles with which they engaged Scripture. While Paul frequently employs the technique of editing violent passages to focus on grace, this is not an approach Jesus often employs (the above example of Jesus removing the wrath from his citation of Isaiah being a notable exception). The approach of Jesus was more often conversational, and typically centered around using paradox or a clever turn of phrase to re-define terms and concepts, turning the tables on his audience's expected perspective.

65

One example of this is Jesus' response to the accusation of working on the Sabbath (punishable by death according to the law). Rather than denying that he is working on the Sabbath, Jesus retorts, "My Father is always at his work to this very day, and I too am working" (John 5:17), thus re-defining his "work" of healing as God's work. This shift is not lost on his audience. As John tells us, "For this reason they tried all the more to kill him because he not only had broken the Sabbath, but said also that God was his Father, making himself equal with God" (v. 18).

The response of Jesus is clearly intended to provoke, and indeed it does. He is publicly and blatantly defying their authority, challenging their interpretation of Scripture. Why does Jesus go out of his way to do this?

Understanding this has everything to do with understanding the way that Jesus read Scripture, in contrast to the way the Pharisees did. While the Pharisees were focused on strict adherence to religious rules and regulations, the priority of Jesus was instead focused on loving and caring for people in need. That is, the way Jesus understood faithfulness to Scripture was that it should lead to love. "Love the Lord your God with all your heart and with all your soul and with all your mind" and "Love your neighbor as yourself," Jesus said. "All the Law and the Prophets hang on these two commandments" (Matt 22:37–40).

For Jesus, the correct interpretation of Scripture all comes down to how we love. The Bible was never intended to be our master, placing a burden on our back; it was intended to act as a servant, leading us to love God, others, and ourselves. When we read it in a way that leads to the opposite of this, we get it wrong. So when the religious leaders interpreted the law in a way that hindered people from finding healing and life, Jesus publicly opposed their hurtful interpretation.

While the particular styles and methods used by Jesus and Paul differ, the common denominator that we can identify as central to how they both interpreted Scripture is this focus on love as the telos of Scripture. This focus has major consequences because it differs quite sharply from the way the vast majority of us have learned to interpret Scripture.

Instead, we are taught to focus on the "correct" reading, paying attention to context, and authorial intent. We seek to find a solid "biblical" view that takes into account all of the data, everything harmonizing and lining up perfectly. This is all well and good in itself. There is nothing wrong with correctly understanding what a text is saying. The problem is when this focus on correct interpretation becomes *primary*, and love takes a backseat, the focus being placed on "being right" and "orthodox" at the expense of love.

This focus on "by the book" interpretation led American Christians in the past to justify the institution of slavery. That may be hard to imagine now since slavery seems so self-evidently immoral to us, but as historian Mark Noll writes, "For over thirty years Americans battled each other exegetically on the issue, with the more orthodox and the ones who took most seriously the authority of Scripture being also the ones most likely to conclude that the Bible sanctioned slavery."[29]

In fact, as Noll illustrates with multiple case studies, it was much easier for those on the pro-slavery side to make a direct appeal to the "common plain meaning" of Scripture. Theirs was the stronger and more self-evident biblical argument. Yet that very focus on "correct" interpretation led them to commit acts of unspeakable cruelty and barbarity—all done in the name of submitting to the authority of Scripture.

Today we can similarly observe how many conservative Christians can become so focused on "right" biblical interpretation that they callously disregard how their position marginalizes and devalues others, leading to people being deeply hurt. This focus of law over love—of scriptural fidelity at the expense of grace—is a direct parallel to the focus of the fundamentalist Pharisees that Jesus so adamantly opposed.

The reason Jesus opposed this way of reading the Bible is the same today as it was then: because it hurts people, hindering them from experiencing God's love and healing. That's the exact opposite of what Scripture is supposed to do. Despite their desire to be "right," these modern-day Christian Pharisees get the Bible dead wrong. As Paul puts it, if we don't have love, all our doctrines and biblical interpretation are just meaningless noise (cf. 1 Cor 13:1–3).

---

29 Mark A. Noll, *The Civil War as a Theological Crisis* (Chapel Hill: University of North Carolina Press, 2006).

In contrast to this Pharisaical approach of prioritizing "being right" over being loving, the focus we observe in Jesus and Paul is on interpreting the biblical text in such a way that it leads to love and compassion. Scripture, when read right, must lead to love. That is the common denominator, the shared bottom line for both Jesus and Paul which shaped how they read. As Paul writes, "Whoever loves others has fulfilled the law. The commandments, 'You shall not commit adultery,' 'You shall not murder,' 'You shall not steal,' 'You shall not covet, and whatever other command there may be, are summed up in this one command: 'Love your neighbor as yourself.' Love does no harm to a neighbor. Therefore love is the fulfillment of the law (Rom 13:8–10). The fulfillment of the law, the fulfillment of Torah, Paul insists, is to love.

Love is the hermeneutical baseline. Paul therefore has no problem with completely misrepresenting a biblical author's intent, and indeed deliberately reverses the meaning of certain passages in order to focus on Christ's way of grace and enemy love. This focus on love and grace was the clear interpretive priority that drove Paul's bold interpretive moves.

While we may not dare to cross out violent passages with our pens as Paul did, we make similar statements with what we choose to highlight and what we don't. Rather than doing this based on what happens to appeal to us personally, as followers of Jesus we need to learn to prioritize what he does. That is precisely what we see Paul doing.

Learning to do this ourselves is not a matter of simply repeating interpretations of specific texts without understanding what led Jesus to make these radical conclusions. We will need to develop a sophisticated understanding of the underlying hermeneutic which led him to make those interpretive moves. The heart of that hermeneutic is understanding that the aim of Scripture is to lead us to love God, others, and ourselves. Nothing could be more central or more crucial to learning to read the Bible like Jesus (and Paul) did.

CHAPTER 4

THE DIVORCE OF ETHICS AND EXEGESIS

We have seen that the way Jesus and Paul interpret Scripture follows in the spirit of faithful questioning motivated by compassion exemplified by the prophetic tradition evidenced throughout the Old Testament itself. How does this compare with how the Christian church has historically interpreted Scripture? For the most part, rather than allowing for questioning and diversity, the focus of the church over the centuries has been on maintaining orthodoxy, labeling those who

71

disagree as heretics. This entails a long history of enforcing its authority through threat of death, torture, exclusion, and hellfire.

We all know about the crusades and inquisition, but even in the Protestant tradition which broke away from the Catholic church, the focus was the same: Their interpretation was in turn viewed as the one and only "right" reading which they likewise enforced through threat of torture and death, executed in God's name. This clearly represents the very worst of the way of *unquestioning obedience* and its inevitable connection to violence committed in God's name. Where did we go so wrong?

It is striking to contrast this violent course taken by the post-Constantinian church with the one that was taken by rabbinical Judaism. Rabbi Anson Laytner makes the case that the tradition of *faithful questioning* is not only typical of the Hebrew Bible, but of the Jewish faith itself. In *Arguing with God: A Jewish Tradition*, Laytner documents the long tradition of Jewish protest. Beginning with examples of protest and questioning in the Hebrew Bible, Laytner continues to trace this pattern of protest within Judaism, citing examples from the Talmud and Midrash, continuing on to the later medieval Jewish prayers of protest known as *Piyyutim*, leading all the way up to the post-holocaust writings of Elie Wiesel.[30] While noting that these voices of protest have often been marginalized by the majority tradition,[31] Rabbi Laytner nevertheless concludes that "argument with God has

---

30 Laytner, *Arguing with God: A Jewish Tradition* (Northvale, NJ: Jason Aronson Inc., 1990).

31 Laytner, *Arguing with God*, 177-178.

persisted as an alternate but recognizable stream of Jewish thought, down through the ages to the modern era."[32]

A key example of this is the Talmud. The Talmud is the written collection of both the Mishnah (the Jewish oral law) and the Gemara, which interprets and comments on the Mishnah. Jews look to the oral law to understand how to interpret the written law (Torah). However, rather than finding a single interpretation informing us of the proper orthodox reading of difficult Torah passages, we instead find in the Talmud a collection of dissenting views of various rabbinic sages presented side by side in a record of discussion and dispute. Like the Old Testament itself, the Talmud is characterized by its collections of multi-vocal debates among the rabbis, giving multiple perspectives on an issue, rather than a single definitive "orthodox" answer. Perhaps this is why it's said that Jewish exegesis is often more comfortable with asking questions than it is with giving answers. After all, the very name "Israel" means "wrestles with God."

From this we can see that a reading of Scripture that *faithfully questions* violence and harm perpetrated in God's name is not only characteristic of Jesus and the New Testament, it's also a deeply Jewish way to read Scripture.

---

32 Laytner, *Arguing with God,* 236. Sounding like the Jewish equivalent of an "emergent" Christian, Laytner complains of how he feels out of place in his experience of contemporary Judaism, and the dilemma this causes for Jews struggling to understand God in a post-holocaust world, "Cut off from the tradition of protest and argument that is the heritage of earlier times, ignorant of the concept of prayer as protest, and deprived of the rich vocabulary of liturgical protest, modern Jews have no outlet to express their darker thoughts to God—certainly not through conventional worship services in a contemporary synagogue or temple" (176).

We see here two diverging trajectories in regards to how to interpret Scripture: The course taken by the church very quickly moved in the direction of *unquestioning obedience*, resulting in staggering acts of violence and inhuman cruelty committed in the name of the faith and in the name of the Bible. In contrast, the course that many contemporary Jews, such as Rabbi Laytner, have come to identify with and see as representative of how their faith interprets Scripture is the way of *faithful questioning*.

For us as Christians who recognize the "wrong turn" the church took in adopting the way of *unquestioning obedience*, this Jewish course of *faithful questioning* holds out the promise of a tradition of biblical interpretation that we may wish to identify with and learn from as well. What might that entail? As Laytner stresses, the voice of *faithful questioning*—whether in the Hebrew Bible or the subsequent trajectory of protest within the Jewish faith—has always been a voice from the margins. It would therefore be a mistake to conclude that there is something inherently good about Jewish culture or inherently bad about Greco-Roman culture—as if there was some magical "biblical" culture that we need to recover.

All cultures, nations, and belief systems are equally prone to error—whether that's the error of the Pharisees or the far greater errors of the Christian church, both of which appealed to Scripture to justify violence. The problem here has nothing to do with a particular culture or religion, and everything to do with the marriage of religion and political power. That is, the key problem is using violence and harm to enforce religious views.

This is always a poisonous combination, and the point at which the church embraced this way is the point where its course diverged from the way of Jesus and the way of love. To truly understand this we will need to take a deeper look at the history of heresy and orthodoxy, and how it developed in the Christian church.

THE GREATEST HERESY

Ironically, the history of heresy began with a concern about religious violence. A popular bishop in the early church named Marcion raised the issue of the problem of violence in the Old Testament, and offered the radical proposal that the entire Old Testament should be rejected because of its immoral image of a violent God which he saw as incompatible with Christ. The early church rejected Marcion's proposal in 144 AD, making Marcion one of the very first people to be labeled as a heretic in Christian history.

Now, there are indeed some genuine problems with Marcion's proposal which become readily apparent in light of the multi-vocal understanding of the Old Testament we have been exploring. When we act as if the Old Testament is all bad or good, we deny that there is in fact diversity and dispute contained within the Hebrew Bible. Positively, we need to instead recognize that truth is not arrived at in the Hebrew canon by silencing dissenting voices or synthesizing them into a cohesive whole, but by allowing each voice to stand on its own along side the other competing voices.

While we can certainly understand the impulse to want to distance oneself from violence in God's name, what is potentially dangerous about Marcion's approach is that it can easily set-up an *us/them* dichotomy where *we* Christians are the good guys with the good book, and *they* (feel free to insert your own enemy here, be it Jews, Muslims, fundamentalists, etc.) are the bad guys with the bad book. So rather than deflecting the blame to some "other" we need to have a way to recognize and deal with the problem of violence in ourselves—in our culture, nation, and faith.

However, if this is Marcion's error then this very error has clearly been perpetuated on a far greater scale by the subsequent post-Constantinian church's focus on enforcing orthodoxy through violence, labeling people as heretics and then persecuting, torturing, and killing them. As we are all sadly aware, this led to unspeakable cruelty and mass murder committed by the church. That is the bitter fruit of the narrative of *unquestioning obedience* within our own Christian history.

Our celebrated First Amendment rights of the freedom of speech and religion in the United States actually came about as a direct response to the church's legacy of persecution and rampant bloodshed. As a result of those Constitutional rights, there are no more burnings at the stake today. However, the spirit of persecuting unorthodoxy still lives on. Many pastors and seminary professors today are fired from their jobs on heresy charges, while others remain silent out of fear of the repercussions to their livelihood.

So again, while I do not subscribe to Marcion's approach, the church's longstanding practice of labeling people as heretics, using this as a weapon to censor, exclude, and harm others is far more grievous and damaging to the faith. After all, what is the greater crime: not getting the formulation of the Trinity quite right, or mass slaughtering those people by the sword? What's the greater sin: questioning a doctrine or working to destroy someone's career and livelihood because they questioned it?

The simple fact is, all the so-called "heresies" throughout history pale in comparison to the hurtful ways that people have been ostracized, threatened, and wounded by those who act as the champions of so-called orthodoxy. The fact that this continues today in this country (albeit without physical violence) is a sad testament to the deadly grip of the authoritarian narrative of *unquestioning obedience* that still drives much of religious belief in America.

Now, let me stress here that the problem is not disagreement in itself. It's understandable when people want to speak out against beliefs or actions that they perceive as hurtful or wrong. Jesus bluntly confronted the Pharisees with their error. Paul was likewise not shy about doing the same with Pharisaical Christians.

The issue is not with disagreeing or with taking moral or theological stands. The issue is with using power and force to harm others. It is a matter of people in positions of power knowingly acting to harm others in order to silence dissent, and doing so believing that this is a shining example of upholding the faith.

What matters far more than the things we profess is *how* we stand up for those convictions. When we do so in a way that wounds, dehumanizes, and harms others this undermines any moral authority we might have had. The greatest heresy, the most dangerous error by far, is the idea that employing force, threat, and violence to silence those who disagree with you is a good and faithful thing to do.

When we act to harm others in the name of orthodoxy or morality we demonstrate that we are neither moral nor orthodox. As Paul says, "Love does no harm to a neighbor. Therefore love is the fulfillment of the law" (Rom 13:10). When we are not acting in love, nothing we do is right, and nothing is orthodox.

DON'T TAKE IT LITERALLY

Now, let's return to Marcion and the response of the early church. There are two things that are critical to note here: The first is that at the time of Marcion heresy was not yet a matter of torturing and killing those who were deemed unorthodox. In contrast to the later church, the early church did not practice violence at all and was instead the target of violent persecution under Rome. The introduction of violence came centuries later, after the church became enmeshed with political power and empire.

What is even more important to note however is that the early church—while disagreeing with Marcion's proposed solution of excising the entire Hebrew Scriptures—very much shared his concern with violence in the Old Testament. This can clearly be seen in the Church Father Origen's response to Marcion: Commenting on the book of Joshua, Origen writes, "Unless those physical wars bore the figure of spiritual wars, I do not think the books of Jewish history would ever have been handed down by the apostles ... who came to teach peace."[33] We can see here that Origen fully recognized the difficulty with the violent image of God that resulted from reading the Old Testament at face value, and consequently rejected that literal reading.

Acknowledging that these Old Testament accounts of war and genocide are "exceedingly difficult"[34] to make sense of morally, Origen insists that we must go beyond the "ordinary usage that speech would indicate" to find the meaning of the Spirit which lies "profoundly buried" beneath it.[35]

---

33 Origen, *Homilies on Joshua* 15.1 in Barbara J. Bruce (Tr.) Cynthia White (Ed.) *The Fathers of the Church: A New Translation, vol. 105, Origen: Homilies on Joshua* (Washington D.C., Catholic University of America Press, 2002), 138.

34 Origen, *De Principiis* 4.9, (ANF 4).

35 Origen, *De Principiis* 4.14, (ANF 4).

When this allegorical method is not applied, Origen tells us, the results are disastrous: Origen complains of the many "simple" but faithful Christians who—like Marcion—seem to have a view of God that "would not be entertained regarding the most unjust and cruel of men."[36] The cause for their monstrous understanding of God, Origen tells us, is because "Holy Scripture is not understood by them according to its spiritual, but according to its literal meaning."[37] Again, what becomes clear from this is that the early church was in fact in agreement with Marcion that the violent picture of God that came from a literal reading was incompatible with Christ, leading people to, as Origen puts it, a view that makes God look worse than "the most unjust and cruel of men."[38]

Rather than simply rejecting the text *in toto* as Marcion did, the solution adopted by Origen and the early church was to employ an allegorical reading of the Old Testament. We can see this same allegorical reading being used today as well when pastors read an Old Testament passage describing war, and then preach a sermon on "fighting the battles" in our own lives. The literal battles in the Bible are used to speak allegorically in their sermon of the spiritual battles in our lives.

Now to be clear, it is not my intent to suggest that we should attempt to revive the early church's allegorical method today. From an ethical perspective the key weakness of the allegorical

---

36 Origen, *De Principiis* 4.8, (ANF 4).

37 Origen, *De Principiis* 4.9, (ANF 4).

38 Origen, *De Principiis* 4.8, (ANF 4).

approach is its tendency to minimize—if not ignore or deny—the problems of violence in the Bible.

For example, when a pastor reads a text promoting genocide in the Old Testament and then proceeds to preach a message on "fighting the battles in our own lives" with no mention of the difficulties the text raises when read in its original historical-grammatical context, this can have the effect of whitewashing over the problem, rather than actually facing it. The unintended result is then sanitizing these violent texts, rather than transforming them.

So while we can appreciate that the early church recognized the need to wrestle with the problem of violence in Scripture, their solution of reading the Old Testament as allegory while failing to face the original violent ethos of these troubling texts is untenable from an ethical perspective, which is at the very heart of Jesus' approach to Scripture.

Re-Thinking Biblical Interpretation

Allegorical reading remained the primary way the church read the Old Testament for centuries, right up to the modern era. In modern times the method of allegorical reading was rejected by biblical scholars, not for ethical reasons, but for academic ones: They objected that it took the biblical passages out of context, projecting a meaning on to them that they did not originally have.

What has been under-appreciated, however, is the ethical reason the church adopted the allegorical method as a way of addressing the problem of violence in Scripture. In other words, when scholarship jettisoned allegorical readings for academic reasons, they lost with it the means to deal with ethical problems in Scripture and offered nothing in its place. As we will see in this section, due to the very definition of how modern exegesis functions, modern biblical scholarship has largely divorced itself from any ethical engagement with the biblical text whatsoever.

The term exegesis comes from a Greek word meaning "to lead out of" and refers to the exposition or explanation of a text based on a careful, objective analysis. The goal here is to approach the text as a scientist, uncovering the evidence, helping us get to what the original author's intent was. We might think here of an archeologist, carefully brushing away the dust from an ancient artifact in order to reveal it to us.

Exegesis is therefore not about evaluating whether a text is good or not. It's simply about accurately reporting the author's intended meaning. Once this is discovered, the interpretive task is to then work out how to apply this in our contemporary context. So the biblical exegete first objectively asks "What does it say?" and then asks "How can we do that?" We might compare this to how the US Supreme Court interprets the intent of the Founding Fathers in the Constitution, applying it to contemporary law.

Now, in and of itself, there is nothing wrong with a historical-grammatical reading of the Bible. It is an important and needed tool. For example, recognizing the way that Paul takes passages out of context in order to disarm them requires that we understand how to read them in context. That is, we can only recognize the continuity and discontinuity between the original passages and Paul's citations because of an awareness of original contexts and meanings. The advantage of modern biblical criticism therefore is that it forces us to face the discrepancy between these Old Testament passages which endorsed "sacred" violence vis-à-vis the subversive readings of Jesus and Paul which acted to "disarm" these texts, converting their original intent away from violence and towards compassion.

At the same time there is a major problem with the modern exegetical method: A mere objective reporting of what a text says in its original context, divorced from any ethical evaluation of its content, is simply not enough if we intend to read Scripture *as Scripture*. Indeed, it is morally irresponsible to stop there. As we have seen, when Jesus and the authors of the New Testament interpret Scripture what they are ultimately doing is an *ethical* evaluation of the text, based on God revealed in Christ. To instead interpret the Old Testament in a way that removes any ethical considerations is to read the Bible in a way that is simply incompatible with the reading of Jesus and Paul.

The core problem therefore with modern biblical interpretation's emphasis on historical-grammatical exegesis is that in its attempt to remain "objective" and scholarly it has consequently divorced itself from any sort of ethical evaluation of the biblical text. In other words, exegesis *by definition* does not involve making any evaluation at all about whether the content of a text is good or not, and instead simply focuses on what it says. Consequently, while biblical scholarship has helped us to understand how to read texts in their proper context, it has for the most part ignored—and in many ways, actively resisted—dealing with the ethical issues raised by these troubling texts, doing so on academic grounds.

To the extent that this is true, it means that biblical scholarship fails to offer any tools with which we can read the Bible morally. This reflects a serious moral flaw in how biblical interpretation has come to be practiced and taught in our seminaries and universities. In an appeal to his fellow scholars, Eryl Davies writes,

> [B]iblical scholars have generally been quite prepared to question the historical accuracy or reliability of the biblical traditions but have shied away from questioning the validity of its moral norms and underlying assumptions. ... As a result, the task of evaluation has all but been evacuated from the realm of biblical criticism. But there must be a place in biblical scholarship—and a respectable and honorable place—for moral critique and ethical appraisal of the biblical tradition. ... It is vital that 'ethical criticism' be placed firmly on the agenda of the university curriculum and that the biblical exegete should be prepared to tackle

what may perhaps be the most important task of the biblical interpreter, namely, that of interacting with the text and reflecting consciously and critically upon the validity or otherwise of its claims.[39]

This has enormous consequences because pastors are taught in seminary that this "objective" method is the "right" way to read their Bibles. When (predominantly liberal and even secular) scholars focus solely on the original meaning of a text as the "right" reading (from the perspective of the "objective" historian), this can easily be taken as validation by conservative apologists that their reading—justifying and sanctifying violence —is the "right" interpretation for Christian application, which in turn affects how we understand God's character, and how we conceive of justice. Teaching exegesis in a way that is intentionally divorced from any sort of moral engagement with the text is to neglect, as Davies says above, the single most important task of the biblical interpreter.

Thankfully, a growing number of scholars like Davies are drawing much needed attention towards bridging this gulf between ethics and biblical scholarship, employing tools such as reader-response criticism which emphasize the importance of

---

39 Eryl W. Davies, "The Morally Dubious Passages of the Hebrew Bible," *Currents in Biblical Research* 3.2 (April 2005), 197-228. 220.

our moral engagement with the text.[40] Their contention is that ethics simply cannot be divorced from exegesis.

The question of how we interpret Scripture, how we apply it to our lives together, is first and foremost a moral question, not an academic one. Because of this, the institutions that train our pastors and biblical scholars need to educate us in how to engage with Scripture ethically, morally, responsibly. Scripture—because of the claim it places on our lives, because it seeks to shape our lives and form how we see our world—simply cannot be approached from a distanced neutrality. We must engage the Bible on an ethical level if we want to read it responsibly, and indeed if we want to read it *as Scripture* at all.

Indeed, Scripture demonstrates this very ethical engagement itself. Throughout both Testaments we can repeatedly observe the biblical authors engaging ethically with Scripture. We see this exemplified in nearly every page of the Psalms, the prophets, and of course Job, all of which, as we have seen, raise moral questions which challenge the law. This engagement is amplified in the examples of Jesus and Paul's reading of Scripture as well which take this ethical critique to a new level. The witness of Scripture models for us, over and over again, that we are likewise called to engage with it ourselves as morally responsible readers.

This does not mean that we should jettison the exegetical method, but rather that it should be understood as a *tool* to help

---

40 For further reading and literature, see Eryl W. Davies, *The Immoral Bible: Approaches to Biblical Ethics* (New York: T&T Clark, 2010). For a helpful example of how reader-response can help facilitate an ethical engagement with troubling violent texts, see Eric A Seibert, *The Violence of Scripture* (Minneapolis: Fortress, 2012).

us in the far more important and central task of reading Scripture ethically *as Scripture*. This entails incorporating the insights of contemporary biblical scholarship into a Christ-centered ethical reading of the Bible. The nuances of such a Christ-centered ethical reading of Scripture will be developed in detail in this book's section on the New Testament. The starting point for that ethical engagement, however, begins with having the simple common sense to recognize that things like infanticide, genocide, and cannibalism are simply and always categorically wrong. Frankly, it does not require a great deal of moral insight to recognize this.

These moral conclusions are easy to make. The real problem is that many of us have been systematically taught in church to shut off our brains and conscience when we read the Bible. In fact, it is commonly taught that we are utterly incapable of making sound moral judgments on our own. Our hearts are "deceitful above all things, and desperately wicked" (Jer 17:9, KJV). We are therefore admonished to "lean not on thine own understanding" (Prov 3:5, KJV), because "God's ways are higher than our ways" (Isa 55:9).[41] These verses are all marshaled to appeal to the narrative of *unquestioning obedience*, and are used to get us to not question moral atrocity in the Bible and instead

---

41 It's worth noting that the original context of this verse is to argue for God's mercy not violence "Let them turn to the LORD, and he will have mercy on them, and to our God, for he will freely pardon. 'For my thoughts are not your thoughts, neither are your ways my ways,' declares the LORD. 'As the heavens are higher than the earth, so are my ways higher than your ways and my thoughts than your thoughts" (Isa 55:7–9).

defend it. The Bible says so; that settles it. End of discussion, end of thought, end of conscience.

In contrast to this hermeneutic of *unquestioning obedience*, we have seen over the last several chapters that the way Jesus read Scripture was instead characterized by a hermeneutic of *faithful questioning* in the name of compassion. Both the hermeneutic of *unquestioning obedience* and the hermeneutic of *faithful questioning* each claim to be the correct way to faithfully interpret Scripture. However, as we have repeatedly seen, one prioritizes compassion over commands, and the other systematically leads to justifying violence and atrocity in God's name. Those are the hard facts, and looking at these it really should be clear that we should choose the "more excellent way" of prioritizing love over law (1 Cor 13).

Jesus—and indeed the very nature of the Hebrew Bible—do not call us into a passive acquiescence to the biblical text. On the contrary, we are compelled to take part in the dispute, to engage with the text ethically. Rather than censoring and sanitizing out the undesirable parts, we are called by the text itself to learn to make ethical evaluations. Rather that being dependent on an authoritarian text, the very disputatious nature of the Hebrew canon invites us to engage with the text in this debate as morally responsible adults.

Faithfulness to Jesus, and to the nature of Scripture itself, requires that we question. As Brueggemann says, "A challenging and revolutionary counter-reading is also permitted, evoked, and legitimated by the text."[42] The multi-vocal nature of the Hebrew Bible invites us to question and wrestle with it. Adopting the way that Jesus and Paul read the Bible, at its most foundational level, is therefore about learning to *think* morally, about learning the virtue of questioning.

---

42 Brueggemann, *Theology of the Old Testament*, 101.

CHAPTER 5

FACING OUR DARKNESS

Thus far we've observed the approach both Jesus and Paul took to interpreting Scripture, characterized by *faithful questioning motivated by compassion*, and how we too are called to enter into this same ethical engagement with Scripture. In this chapter we now turn to application, facing some of the most troubling texts found in the Hebrew Bible and exploring how we might nevertheless approach these as Scripture without whitewashing over the very real ethical difficulties they present.

DIVIDING THE DEMONIC
FROM THE DIVINE

Looking at the record of dispute found throughout the Old Testament, we can begin to trace the outlines of a people's slow development away from the primitive view of violent tribal war gods so typical of the worldview of the ancient world. Part of this development involved Judaism moving from polytheism to monotheism. However, an unfortunate byproduct of this shift to monotheism involved their attributing both good *and* evil acts to God. In the strictly monotheistic view of the Old Testament, all actions—both evil and good—were done by the sole actor Yahweh.

> "When disaster comes to a city, has not the LORD caused it?
> (Amos 3:6).

> "I form the light and create darkness, I bring prosperity and create disaster; I, the LORD, do all these things."
> (Isaiah 45:7)

The word translated here as "disaster" in these above two passages is literally "evil" in Hebrew. "When *evil* comes to a city, has not the LORD caused it?" In their ancient mindset disaster and injury were understood as evil, and God was seen as the author of both good and evil. Elsewhere in the Old Testament we similarly see God portrayed as deceiving and hardening the hearts of people:

> "So now, look, the LORD has placed a lying spirit in the mouths of all these prophets of yours, but the LORD has decreed disaster for you." (1 Kings 22:23)

Again, the word translated "disaster" above in the NIV is literally "evil" in Hebrew. So this verse makes the morally troubling assertion that God "has decreed evil for you" by causing the prophets to lie.

By the time of Jesus, later Judaism had developed away from this view towards a more complex understanding which recognized that bad things can happen which are not God's will, and instead disaster and death were attributed to the devil.

Consequently, many of the violent acts which the Old Testament portrays as God's doing, Jesus and the New Testament instead attribute to the work of Satan. A prominent example of this is sickness which the Old Testament attributes to God's will as a just punishment for sin, but Jesus instead attributes to "the work of the devil" which he consequently does not affirm as God's righteous judgment, but rather actively opposes in God's name.

This development—moving away from the view that God causes evil (rape, famine, sickness, war), towards a view that such evil is demonic—can be seen much earlier within Judaism in the intertestamental book of Jubilees (ca. 100 BCE) which revises the biblical narratives found in Genesis and the beginning of Exodus. The book of Jubilees takes many passages, which in the Old Testament books are attributed to God, and instead states that these were in fact the work of "Mastema," the prince of demons.

For example, while Exodus says that God killed the firstborn children in Egypt (Exod 11:4), the later book of Jubilees instead attributes this to "the powers of *Mastema*" which literally means in Hebrew "the powers of *Hate*" (Jubilees 49:2). This illustrates the shift in thinking that was occurring within Judaism at the time which recognized the obvious moral difficulty in attributing acts of evil to God.

We can see a similar revisionism as well in the canonical books of the Old Testament itself. 2 Samuel describes God telling David to take a census, and then punishing him for it: "Again the anger of the LORD burned against Israel, and he incited David against them, saying, 'Go and take a census of Israel and Judah'" (2 Sam 24:1). David then subsequently recognizes that this was a sin: "David was conscience-stricken after he had counted the fighting men, and he said to the LORD, 'I have sinned greatly in what I have done'" (v. 10). God then punishes David for this: "So the LORD sent a plague on Israel from that morning until the end of the time designated, and seventy thousand of the people from Dan to Beersheba died" (v. 15).

This obviously paints a morally problematic picture of God, which is revised in the parallel account in the later book of 1 Chronicles, which instead states, "Satan rose up against Israel and incited David to take a census of Israel" (1 Chron 21:1). Instead of God deceiving David and inciting him to sin, this is now presented as the work of Satan.

While the concept of the devil is rare in the Old Testament, by the time of Jesus it was a common feature within Judaism. What is significant here is the ethical implications of this shift in perspective. Rather than blaming people for their sufferings, the response of Jesus was to recognize that God is not the author of evil, and that consequently our response should be one of compassion and care. Suffering is not to be affirmed as God's will, it is to be opposed in the name of love.

From this perspective, when we read passages that ascribe evil to God in the Old Testament, we need to recognize that this is written from the viewpoint of a people who had no concept of the devil, and who consequently attributed injury, deception, and suffering to the hand of God.

When we therefore read accounts of God commanding moral atrocities such as genocide in the Old Testament, we need to ask ourselves whether this might more accurately be seen—from the perspective of Jesus—as in fact describing the work of Satan and not God. Frankly, it is hard to imagine something more demonic than commanding people to commit genocide.[43]

---

43 Recall as well the passage cited in chapter two where Jesus rejects the suggestion of his disciples that he follow the example of Elijah and call down fire from heaven,

GOD SAID IT,
BUT THAT DOESN'T SETTLE IT

It is easy to recognize a clear difference between the earlier descriptions in the Old Testament which attribute evil and deception to God, and the later understanding of Second Temple Judaism seen in the New Testament. It is important, however, to remember that the Hebrew Bible itself provides us with a record of this developing dispute.

We have already seen several examples from the Psalms, prophets, and Job of people arguing with God in the Old Testament—in each case questioning the legitimacy of suffering and violence attributed to God's will. However, we can find something even more surprising within the multi-vocal Hebrew canon:

Not only do we find examples of humans arguing with God, we also find examples of God arguing with God.

That is, we find within the Old Testament the direct words of God proclaimed by the prophets contradicted by the direct words of God proclaimed by other prophets, again reflecting how central dispute is to the character of the Hebrew Bible.

For example, the law declares that God takes pleasure in destroying people, while the prophets, in contrast, emphatically state that the opposite is the case. In Deuteronomy we read, "Just

---

telling them that they are thinking like the devil: "You do not realize what spirit you are of."

as it pleased the LORD to make you prosper and increase in number, *so it will please him* to ruin and destroy you" (Deut 28:63). Yet Ezekiel declares, "As surely as I live, declares the Sovereign LORD, *I take no pleasure* in the death of the wicked!" (Ezek 33:11). In one account God takes pleasure in destruction, and in another this is emphatically denied. "As surely as I live, declares the Sovereign LORD."

Similarly, we read in the law the declaration that God punishes sons for their father's sins: "I, the LORD your God, am a jealous God, punishing the children for the sin of the fathers" (Exod 20:5; Deut 5:9). This is stated as a direct quote from God.

We later read how such "inherited" punishment is said to have been carried out as a consequence for King David's sins. Nathan prophesies to David, "Because by doing this you have shown utter contempt for the LORD, the son born to you will die" (2 Sam 12:14).

The text goes on to describe a father's anguish. "David pleaded with God for the child. He fasted and spent the nights lying in sackcloth on the ground" (v. 16). But David's prayers were not heard. Instead, we are told that "the Lord struck the child" (v. 15) with sickness, and he soon died. So in this account King David sins, and God kills his little boy. "I, the LORD your God, am a jealous God, punishing the children for the sin of the fathers!" Thus saith the Lord.

In contrast to this, the prophet Ezekiel directly contradicts this principle, declaring, "As surely as I live, declares the Sovereign

LORD, you will no longer quote this proverb in Israel" (Ezek 18:3). His prophecy continues, "He will not die for his father's sin; he will surely live ... The son will not share the guilt of the father, nor will the father share the guilt of the son" (v. 17, 19). "As surely as I live, declares the Sovereign LORD." Here we have a statement placed directly in the mouth of God, confronting and contradicting the previous declaration of the Lord in the law.

Each of these above contradictory statements claim to speak for God in no uncertain terms. In one God is said to kill children for the sins of their parents. In the other God is said to emphatically deny this. Is this an example of God's character changing? I doubt that anyone would want to argue that. A much more obvious and likely conclusion is that we have here a record of dispute and disagreement between the law and the prophets—each claiming to truly speak for God, each declaring "thus saith the Lord."

These are not examples of unintended contradictions. Rather, they are *intentional* contradictions, a record of the dispute found throughout the Hebrew canon, cataloging developing and conflicting views of God. Therefore, rather than viewing such contradictions as something embarrassing we need to explain away, we can instead view them positively as a record of moral development that emerges through dispute and protest.

Now, it's important to acknowledge here that the Old Testament was not composed with the intent of being an open debate, as if both sides agreed to respectfully make room for the other to be heard. Instead, the majority voice on the side of *unquestioning obedience* sought to enforce its view alone through violent threat. There is no intention here of allowing for other voices of dissent to be heard. *Obey or else, no questions asked.* This is the ethos of the majority narrative of *unquestioning obedience.*

Yet in the canon of the Hebrew Bible we nevertheless find these minority voices of protest, examples of *faithful questioning* included alongside the majority view. The fact that the minority voice managed to find a place in the canon alongside the majority voice says something remarkable about the Jewish faith that we as Christians really need to learn from. For it is by listening to these minority voices, speaking from the margins— giving a voice to the victims of religious scapegoating violence— that we can become aware of how our own interpretations and theology, intended for good, can become hurtful. When we can learn to hear these protests from the margins this leads us to reform and compassion.

What we can observe in these particular examples is that this way of faithful questioning extends even to statements attributed directly to God in the Bible. Even when we find these "thus saith the Lord" statements we are forced to deliberate between these conflicting claims.

Logically, we cannot accept two mutually contradictory statements. We must make a choice. The multi-vocal nature of the Bible means that the biblical canon—by including these conflicting views—forces us to deliberate, to morally engage with these statements, rather than passively accept them unthinkingly.

With this in mind, recall the divine commands to commit genocide noted in chapter one. "This is what the Lord Almighty says ... attack the Amalekites ... Do not spare them; put to death men and women, children and infants" (1 Sam 15:2-3). This passage is particularly challenging because it is stated as a direct command from God. However, as we have seen above, prophets such as Ezekiel challenged and contradicted such direct "thus saith the Lord" statements with their own insisting counter-witness, spoken with the same voice of divine authority.

Ezekiel contradicts Samuel above on punishing sons for the sins of their fathers. Could Ezekiel not also equally contradict Samuel here as well? If Ezekiel might do this, then can we, following in the same way of *faithful questioning* that Jesus models for us and calls us to take up in the name of compassion for the least, for the little ones?[44]

---

44 A similar example can be found in Jeremiah who prophesies in the name of the Lord, "I never commanded—nor did it enter my mind—that they should do such a detestable thing!" (Jer 32:35) referring to the practice of child sacrifice which the Israelites had adopted. Many examples of this can be found in the OT, although by the time the OT was edited together their beliefs had shifted away from this practice so most of it was likely redacted and we only find the "tip of the iceberg." Some examples that linger are the story of Abraham and Issac (which many read as a pivotal story marking the Israelites moving away from this practice of child sacrifice), commands to offer up the firstborn son as a "ransom" in the law, and stories like that of Jephthah's daughter. Jeremiah is thus referring to a practice that was a core part of Israelite religious life in the past, and presumably prevalent enough at the time that Jeremiah felt the need to confront it, and reject their view that this was what God had commanded.

Scholars have similarly noted that the divine commands to commit genocide (known as the *herem*, often translated as "devoted to destruction") can likewise be understood as a form of human sacrifice. Therefore Jeremiah's rebuke of child sacrifice has a direct connection to the related practice of "devoting people to the Lord" in the form of genocidal slaughter—both of which reflected common perspectives in the surrounding cultures of the ancient world that the ancient Israelites, emerging out of that same culture, had likewise embraced as God's will. For a study of this, see Susan

Perhaps someone might object here that Ezekiel had a special insider right as a prophet to contradict other prophetic utterances elsewhere in Scripture; we, however, cannot. But are we not in fact *more* qualified than Ezekiel to boldly make these calls, since we know Christ? Do we not in fact have a superior revelation of God's true nature in Jesus, and through the indwelling Holy Spirit?

This is in fact precisely what Paul claims for us. Addressing the church, he declares "The person with the Spirit makes judgments about all things" (1 Cor 2:15). These judgments, Paul explains, can even involve standing up to the prophets. To demonstrate this Paul quotes from Isaiah who thunders, "Who has known the mind of the Lord so as to instruct him!?" implying that we cannot question (1 Cor 2:16 quoting Isaiah 40:13).

However, rather than agreeing with the prophet's authority, Paul instead defiantly shoots back in response to Isaiah the retort: "But *we* have the mind of Christ!" (v. 17). While Isaiah effectively cries out "Who dares to challenge the Bible?" Paul answers defiantly "We who have the mind of Christ, that's who!" The way of *faithful questioning* not only authorizes us to question and challenge Scripture in the name of compassion as Jesus and Paul both do—it obligates us to question because this is what it means to take a stand for love, this is what faithfulness looks like.

Niditch, *War in the Hebrew Bible: A Study in the Ethics of Violence* (Oxford, Oxford University Press, 1995), 28–55.

101

Fantasies of Genocide

Because the Hebrew Bible is multi-vocal, consequently some of it gets God right, and some of it gets God terribly wrong. In light of this, it is not terribly surprising to discover that extensive archeological findings in the later part of the 20th century have convinced the vast majority of scholars today that the genocide accounts recorded in the book of Joshua are largely fictional.

For example, beginning in the 1950s, advances in archeology allowed Kathleen Kenyon to argue that Jericho was destroyed more than a century before Joshua ever got there. More recently, high-precision radiocarbon dating has confirmed Kenyon's findings.[45] Thus Robert Hubbard writes, "The current scholarly consensus follows the conclusion of Kenyon... Jericho was completely uninhabited circa 1550–1100 BCE. In other words, notwithstanding Joshua 6, there was no fortified city of Jericho for Joshua and Israel to conquer."[46]

As Archeologist William Dever notes, other cities that were supposedly wiped out according to the biblical accounts show no archeological evidence of destruction whatsoever. Dever therefore concludes, "There is little that we can salvage from Joshua's stories of the rapid, wholesale destruction of Canaanite

---

45 H.J. Bruins and J. van der Plicht, "Tell es-Sultan (Jericho): Radiocarbon results of short-lived cereal and multiyear charcoal samples from the end of the Middle Bronze Age" *Radiocarbon* 37/2 (1995), 213–20.

46 Robert L. Hubbard Jr., *Joshua: The NIV Application Commentary* (Grand Rapids: Zondervan, 2009) 203.

cities and the annihilation of the local population. It simply did not happen; the archeological evidence is indisputable."[47]

Now, that is not to say that there were no wars, no violence committed in the name of God at the time. This was clearly a brutally violent era. However, it does raise an important question for us:

If the genocide accounts are in fact a fiction—a conclusion that the archeological evidence clearly points towards—this obviously would imply that the claim that God commanded them is equally a fiction.

God never said to destroy Jericho, not only because God is not a war criminal, but because Jericho was long empty at the time. The same is true for the city of Ai which literally means "ruins." Who names a city "ruins" unless it already is one? As the archeological evidence shows, this was exactly the case when they got there.[48]

While it is certainly a relief to learn that the biblical genocide accounts were in all likelihood a fiction (which makes it much easier to recognize that the claim that God would command such a thing is equally a fiction) this does not change the fact that the violent ideology behind them is clearly deplorable. Nor does it change the indisputable reality that this very ideology has been used to justify very real historical genocide and bloodshed in the

---

47 William Dever, *Who Were the Early Israelites and Where Did They Come From* (Grand Rapids: Eerdmans, 2003), 228.

48 Dever, *Who Were the Early Israelites*, 47–48. See also Robert L. Hubbard Jr., "Ai" in Bill T. Arnold, H. G. M. Williamson (eds.) *Dictionary of the Old Testament: Historical Books* (Downers Grove: Intervarsity, 2005), 21–22.

name of God ever since—genocide perpetrated by the Christian church no less. That is the fruit of reading the Bible unquestioningly.

FACING OUR DARKNESS

So, given all of this, what would it mean to read Scripture—and in particular these troubling Old Testament texts—*as Scripture?*

The place where this must start is with our ethical engagement with the text. Evaluating the moral claims of Scripture based on how it reflects Christ-likeness can be a complex and difficult task. However, there are some cases where it is not so difficult. For example, it does not take a great deal of moral insight to recognize that genocide is wrong or that it is not "blessed" to smash a toddler's head against a rock.[49] There is a clear incompatibility between Jesus and genocide.

Therefore, rather than attempting to justify or explain such passages we need to face these violent parts of the Old Testament, owning them as part of our own religious history, while clearly acknowledging them as morally unacceptable. This is where we must start, with an unambiguous rejection of these texts. We need to recognize that they are reflective of a primitive

---

49 Duh.

and morally inferior understanding of God that Judaism itself gradually developed away from.

However, once we have done this, the next question becomes: What do we do with these "texts of terror"? Should we simply toss them out as Marcion proposed? Unfortunately, this has become the de facto strategy most of us have adopted. We have thus inadvertently become "de facto-Marcionites" because we simply avoid reading these deeply troubling parts of Scripture at all—effectively creating our own personal "canon within the canon" of texts we focus on, and texts we prefer to ignore.

This tendency is reflected in the common lectionaries of the Catholic and Mainline Protestant churches which have systematically removed violent passages from their readings.[50] In many ways, of course this can be seen as a positive move. I'm frankly glad most people don't underline and highlight the gruesome accounts of bloodshed and suffering in their Bibles. But ignoring a problem does not make it go away. We need to shine light on it, not cover it up.

Instead of ignoring these troubling texts, we need to have the courage to face them honestly, and to consider the ethical problems they clearly raise. This may involve discussing how the assumptions of religious violence in a text have found their way into our own values and assumptions.

It's also helpful to view these texts from the perspective of the victim, as Jesus so often did. We might, for example, try to read

---

50 See Philip Jenkins, *Laying Down the Sword: Why We Can't Ignore the Bible's Violent Verses* (New York: HarperOne, 2011), 202–8.

the Exodus story from the perspective of the conquered Canaanites, or view the story of the flood from outside of the ark.[51] Finally, we need to ask how Christ and his way of compassion, grace, and enemy love might point to better Jesus-shaped alternatives to the ones found in such passages.[52]

While we may be tempted to simply write off the Old Testament as the product of a primitive people (and indeed, justifying genocide is undeniably reflective of a primitive and inferior morality), it would equally be naive for us to deny our own susceptibility to the seduction of violence today in the name of "justice."

While we need to begin with an unambiguous rejection of the ideology of violence and dehumanization in these troubling texts, we must at the same time allow them to reveal our own blinders as well. So the best thing we can do is allow these texts to give us insight into our own lives so we can honestly face the darkness and pain there, and find ways of breaking out of the deadly logic of justifying violence ourselves.

Consider the shocking "anti-beatitude" of Psalm 137, "Blessed is the one who seizes your infants and dashes them against the rocks!" While we must begin by clearly stating that it is certainly not "blessed" to kill toddlers, as this psalm disturbingly proclaims, if we can step back and view these words

---

51 On this, see the now famous article by Robert Allan Warrior, "Canaanites, Cowboys and Indians" *Christianity and Crisis* 49 (1989), 261-65.

52 For more detail on these and other helpful strategies for ethically wrestling with violence in Scripture, see Eric Seibert, *The Violence of Scripture* (Minneapolis: Fortress, 2012).

from a human perspective—and, indeed, all of the Psalms are passionately written from that very raw human vantage point—then we can hear in these disturbing words the desperate cry of one who is suffering and in grief. This grief is indicated in the psalm's opening line, "By the rivers of Babylon we sat and wept!" (Psalm 137:1).

This psalm is a cry of angry grief, showing us that we can likewise come to God with that same kind of raw honesty, with our doubts, our grief, and even our rage. Consider these painful words from the book of Job:

> God has turned me over to the ungodly and thrown me into the clutches of the wicked … He has made me his target … God has wronged me. (Job 16:11-12; 19:6)

> I cry to you, O God, but you don't answer. I stand before you, but you don't even look.
> You have become cruel toward me. You use your power to persecute me. (Job 30:20-21 NLT)

Job's friends rebuke him for these accusations, but in the end, God rebukes Job's friends, saying, "You have not spoken the truth about me, as my servant Job has" (Job 42:7–8). Now, surely this does not mean that God affirming being "wrong" and "cruel" as Job accuses, but rather that God respects Job's honest cry of pain over the somber apologetics of his friends.

Once we recognize this, we can likewise read Psalm 137 with sympathy, while at the same time not condoning it. What we discover, when we step back and recognize the human voice behind the psalm, is that this is not a divine oracle condoning infanticide. Rather, it is the honest expression of human anguish —the cry of someone who has suffered horrific violence and injustice.

Even in their anger and ugliness, passages like these show us that we can be real and raw with God. We can have the courage to let Jesus into the brokenness of our lives, the courage to be loved for who we really are. That's what faith is about: It's not about certainty, it's about vulnerability. It is the outrageous hope that we would still be loved if God knew about all the ugly things we try to hide.

With this perspective in mind, let's consider the popular Psalm 139. This classic psalm is widely recognized as a beautiful and poetic expression of intimacy with God,

> You have searched me, LORD, and you know me.
> You know when I sit and when I rise;
>   you perceive my thoughts from afar.
> You discern my going out and my lying down;
>   you are familiar with all my ways.
> Before a word is on my tongue
>   you, LORD, know it completely.
> You hem me in behind and before,
>   and you lay your hand upon me.

Such knowledge is too wonderful for me,
 too lofty for me to attain.

Where can I go from your Spirit?
 Where can I flee from your presence?
If I go up to the heavens, you are there;
 if I make my bed in the depths, you are there.
If I rise on the wings of the dawn,
 if I settle on the far side of the sea,
even there your hand will guide me,
 your right hand will hold me fast.
If I say, "Surely the darkness will hide me
 and the light become night around me,"
even the darkness will not be dark to you;
 the night will shine like the day,
 for darkness is as light to you.

For you created my inmost being;
 you knit me together in my mother's womb.
I praise you because I am fearfully and wonderfully made;
 your works are wonderful,
 I know that full well.

My frame was not hidden from you
 when I was made in the secret place,
 when I was woven together in the depths of the earth.
Your eyes saw my unformed body;
 all the days ordained for me were written in your book

109

before one of them came to be.
How precious to me are your thoughts, God!
How vast is the sum of them!
Were I to count them,
  they would outnumber the grains of sand—
when I awake, I am still with you.

                                      (Psalm 139:1–18)

This is where the reading stops in most liturgies, and also where the highlighting stops in most of our Bibles. But the psalm continues with this disturbing prayer:

If only you, God, would slay the wicked!
  Away from me, you who are bloodthirsty!
They speak of you with evil intent;
  your adversaries misuse your name.
Do I not hate those who hate you, LORD,
  and abhor those who are in rebellion against you?
I have nothing but hatred for them;
  I count them my enemies.

Search me, God, and know my heart;
  test me and know my anxious thoughts.
See if there is any offensive way in me,
  and lead me in the way everlasting.

                                      (Psalm 139:19–24)

Here we read a prayer request for God to "kill the wicked" (v. 19), and the psalmist's declaration of his "perfect hatred" presented to God as a virtue. The psalm ends with the petition "Search me, God, and know my heart ... *See if there is any offensive way in me*" (v. 23–24). Given the previous verses' disturbing proclamations of hatred and death wishes, this must strike us as painfully ironic.

Without question there is a clear conflict here with Jesus' command to love our enemies. The "offense" is right there in the previous verses, but the psalmist doesn't see it, and instead thinks of it as a virtue.

The fact that we find these disturbing words intertwined into the middle of a psalm of such stirring beauty and intimacy makes it all the more challenging. It would be so much easier if we could just find the "bad" books or the "bad" psalms and remove them; but here we have hatred right in the middle of a prayer of trust and devotion, woven into one of the most cherished psalms in Scripture.

This serves as a mirror into our own hearts and lives which are likewise characterized by good and bad, beauty and ugliness. As Solzhenitsyn famously said, speaking out of his experience in the brutal and soul-crushing Russian gulag:

> If only there were evil people somewhere insidiously committing evil deeds, and it were necessary only to separate them from the rest of us and destroy them. But the line dividing good and evil cuts through the heart of every

111

human being. And who is willing to destroy a piece of his own heart?[53]

Just as the line dividing good and evil cuts through the heart of every human being, it also cuts right through the middle of Psalm 139, reflecting our human hearts before God in all of their beauty—and in all of their darkness as well. We can no more cut out these verses than we can cut out a piece of our own hearts. Instead, we need to learn how to honestly face this in the Bible, just as we must learn to honestly face it in ourselves.

The true beauty of the Hebrew Bible is that it welcomes and makes room for diversity, and for the marginal voices to be heard. We honor this by entering ourselves into an ethical reading and critical engagement with the text.

This involves our questioning and challenging the Bible, but it equally involves allowing ourselves to be challenged and stretched by it as well. It demonstrates that truth is found in the struggle together—that questioning is the mark of a healthy faith, and the reflection of a robust character. To honor this in Scripture, we need to learn to approach the Bible not as passive readers, but as morally engaged and thinking readers. That is the hermeneutic of *faithful questioning*.

---

53 Aleksandr Solzhenitsyn, *The Gulag Archipelago* (New York, Harper Perennial Modern Classics, 2002), 75.

PART II:

VIOLENCE AND THE NEW TESTAMENT

CHAPTER 6

READING ON A TRAJECTORY

In this section we move from an exploration of the problem of violence in the Old Testament to looking at the issue of violence in the New Testament. There is undeniably a marked difference between the two testaments in regards to violence, that even the most casual observer is quick to recognize. While the Old Testament contains repeated commands for God's people to commit genocidal slaughter, in contrast there are no commands in the New Testament for people to kill anyone at all (let alone commands to commit genocide). On the contrary, the way of retribution is explicitly forbidden in the New Testament, and followers of Jesus are called to the way of nonviolent enemy love and radical forgiveness (the extent of which we Christians have been faithful to that calling is another matter).

We can observe in this a clear and undeniable break between the two testaments in regards to violence committed in God's name which has profound ethical consequences that can hardly be overstated: In one, human violence committed in God's name is a central theme, in the other it is categorically rejected as unacceptable for the people of God.

Nevertheless, there are a number of issues in the New Testament in regards to the legitimation of violence that will be important to address. Over the next several chapters we will thus explore a number of these core issues, including how the New Testament has been (mis)used to justify the institution of slavery, corporal punishment of children, and the legitimation of state violence in the form of war and the punishment of crime, including capital punishment.

This initial chapter will set the stage for that larger discussion by outlining a general approach to how to interpret the New Testament, understanding it in its original context and how this applies normatively in our contemporary context today.

Before we do this however it's important to step back and appreciate the major changes that had taken place within Judaism in the many centuries that had passed between where the Old Testament leaves off and where the New Testament begins. Understanding these changes in circumstance and how they affected developing beliefs will help us understand the context within which the New Testament was written, and its radical message of grace and enemy love.

A HISTORY OF SUFFERING

Israel's founding story was the exodus where God liberated the Israelites from bondage in Egypt and brought them into the promised land. The covenant made between the Israelites and God was that if they remained faithful they would succeed in war and flourish as a nation.

However, at the time of the prophets, the Israelites found themselves in captivity again, this time to Babylon. They were a people in exile, a besieged and oppressed nation longing to return to their former glory. The message of the prophets was to tell this oppressed people that the reason for their suffering and defeat was not because God had abandoned them (as many of the Psalms and the book of Job claim in a counter-narrative), but because Israel had sinned. The reason they were starving and oppressed, the reason their mother or daughter was raped, say the prophets, was because they had been unfaithful.

You may ask yourself, 'Why is all this happening to me?' Because of your many sins! That is why you have been stripped and raped by invading armies ... This is your

allotment, the portion I have assigned to you, says the Lord,
For you have forgotten me, putting your trust in false gods. I
myself will strip you and expose you to shame! (Jer 13:22,
25, NLT)

The prophets promise that if Israel would repent, they would
be restored and find themselves ruling over all of the gentile
nations. This is described in terms of a violent military victory,
and consequently many looked for the messiah to be a warrior
king who would vanquish Israel's oppressors and restore justice.

Israel in fact did repent, but the promised glorious return
from exile never came. The book of Ezra records the return to
Jerusalem, the rebuilding of the temple, and national repentance.
However, this took place while under Persian rule. Israel never
was restored to its former glory, nor was it victorious over its
enemies. Instead, they endured many centuries of oppression,
and—as one oppressive nation succeeded another—that hope for
a return to Israel's former glory grew ever dimmer. First under
oppressive Assyrian rule, then Babylon, then Persia, then Greece,
and then finally—centuries later in the time of Jesus—the
Roman occupation where they continued to be a captive and
oppressed people. Israel was passed on as the spoils of war from
one successive occupying power to the next.

The message of the prophets can be understood as a theodicy
—a way of making sense of their suffering. But that explanation
came at a high price. It entailed both a blaming of the victim, as
well as a disturbing emphasis on anger in God's character. The

prophets soften this by stating that God's anger will not endure forever, promising that everything will be restored. But when the oppression instead continued, for generation after generation, and century upon century, it becomes questionable how long the heavy burden of such an explanation can remain tenable to a suffering people. As Jack Miles writes:

> If God must be defined as a historical-time, physical-world warrior whose victory has simply been postponed indefinitely, then there might as well be no such god. Indefinite postponement is tantamount to cancelation. Effectively, after such a conclusion, the only choices left are atheism or some otherwise unthinkably radical revision in the understanding of God.[54]

That "radical revision in the understanding of God" came in Christ. By the time of the New Testament, after centuries of oppression, being passed as the spoils of war from one occupying power to the next, it was understandable that many Jews were ready to re-think the narrative which blamed the victims.

After centuries of oppression, the identity of God as a conquering war god had simply become untenable. This was a narrative which can be sustained so long as one is part of a conquering nation, but for a people who have been displaced and oppressed for centuries, that war god increasingly looks like an empty promise.

---

54 Jack Miles, *Christ: A Crisis in the Life of God* (New York: Vintage Books, 2001), 117.

Jesus instead comes and proposes a very different narrative and understanding of who God is. Those who are suffering, sick, and victimized are not being punished by God for their sins; they are under Satan's bondage and need to be set free. Salvation does not come through a warrior messiah who brings military victory through violent conquest, as many of the prophets predicted. Rather, the messiah preaches military renunciation, calling instead for forgiveness and love of enemies. Salvation comes on the cross by the messiah suffering unjust violence, not inflicting it. The enemy is not another nation; the enemy is the devil, and the recipient of God's salvation is again not a single nation, but the whole world.

Thus the New Testament not only joins in the Hebrew tradition of faithful questioning of sacred violence, it proposes a new nonviolent vision of who God is and what salvation looks like. The warrior God has become the suffering God. God has been disarmed because Jesus reveals the true heart of the Father. God does not look like a warrior king clothed in the blood of his enemies; God instead looks like Jesus, clothed in his own blood, shed for his enemies. God has not changed; rather, Jesus reveals to us who God has always been. Scripture is only read right when it is read in a way that leads us to a Jesus-shaped life and a Jesus-shaped understanding of God's heart.

A CHANGE IN COURSE

The New Testament constitutes a radical revision of who God is and how salvation comes about which directly confronts the dominant narrative of violence that had saturated the imagination of both the Jewish and Greco-Roman culture at the time. Most significant here is not simply Jesus' focus on God's love and care for the oppressed and marginalized, but more radically his message of God's love of enemies.

Consequently, in contrast to the majority narrative of the Old Testament which had shaped the messianic expectations of the people, Jesus does not understand violence as a means for bringing about God's justice and salvation, but instead calls his followers to renounce violence, demonstrating that way of nonviolent enemy love on the cross.

The New Testament is therefore a protest-narrative constituting a major critique of religiously justified violence. But it is more than this: It goes beyond mere critique and protest, and articulates a radical alternative way, characterized by forgiveness and enemy love. This is the core narrative of the New Testament.

In a later chapter we will explore a practical approach to the application of enemy love today, both on a personal and societal level. Before we get to practical application in our contemporary context, however, we need to begin with our approach to interpretation, outlining how that approach functions, how it differs from a "plain reading" of Scripture, and why this difference is so important in regards to violence.

We do not find in the pages of the New Testament the final and ultimate picture of this alternate way of enemy love, but instead a record of the first bold and faithful steps taken in that direction within their own cultural context and time which was engulfed in the assumption that violence is virtuous.

The New Testament is therefore a book that needs to be understood within its own religious and cultural context. It cannot be read in isolation, as if it were a timeless document of rules from God that fell out of the sky into our laps in the 21st century. Rather it is a reaction to the religious and cultural world in which it found itself in. It is a protest-narrative born out of a religious past that had a long history of justifying violence in God's name.

To understand the New Testament we need to understand that religious past, in order to recognize what it is protesting *against*. Properly interpreting the New Testament—not as detached scholars but as followers of Jesus and his way—thus involves recognizing the redemptive trajectory it sets away from religious violence, and then continuing to develop and move forward along that same trajectory ourselves. In other words, *we cannot stop at the place the New Testament got to, but must recognize where it was headed.*

A clear example of this can be seen in the institution of slavery: The New Testament takes major steps away from slavery, encouraging slaves to gain their freedom if possible (1 Cor 7:21), counseling masters to treat their slaves as Christ treats them (Eph 6:9), and, most significantly, declaring that in Christ there is "no slave or free," that is, no concept of class or superiority (Gal 3:28).

While we can recognize here a movement away from slavery that set a trajectory which would eventually lead to the complete abolition of the institution of slavery centuries later, we do not see the New Testament directly condemning slavery or calling for its abolishment. Masters are not told to give up their slaves as Christians, but simply to treat them well. Slaves are not encouraged to participate in an "underground railroad" to gain their freedom, but instead are told to submit—even in the face of the cruelty, oppression, and violence that characterized slavery in the ancient Greco-Roman world at the time.

If we read the New Testament as a storehouse of eternal principles, representing a "frozen in time" ethic, where we can simply flip open a page and find what the timeless "biblical" view on any particular issue is—as so many people read the Bible today—then we would need to conclude that the institution of slavery has God's approval in the New Testament, and that we should therefore support and maintain it today. This is in fact *exactly* how many American slave-owning Christians did read the Bible in the past. Yet all of us would agree today that slavery is immoral. So how can we understand the New Testament witness here?

This is where the importance of a trajectory reading comes in. William Webb has proposed that we must learn to recognize the redemptive direction that Scripture is moving in, and differentiate this from the cultural assumptions of the time. In the following diagram we can see how Webb's "redemptive movement hermeneutic" functions:[55]

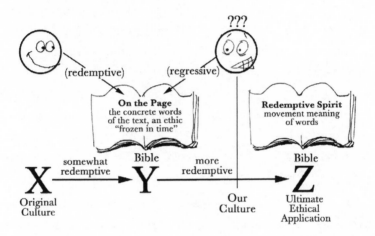

Note the dispositions of the happy face on the left, and the *not-so-happy face* on the right. From within the context of the original culture "X" the concrete words of Scripture "Y" represents a positive but less-than-ultimate redemptive movement forward. However, looking back from our own time, those same words can seem regressive. To read it right, we must therefore learn to recognize the "redemptive spirit" of the text leading us

---

55 Modified diagram adapted from William Webb, *Corporal Punishment in the Bible: A Redemption Movement-Hermeneutic for Troubling Texts* (Downers Grove, IVP Academic, 2011), 59.

to continue to move with God's Spirit along the trajectory this sets towards an ultimate ethical application "Z".

A critical aspect of this model involves recognizing that the New Testament itself does not represent an ultimate ethic, but instead is representative of the first steps in that new direction. We need to recognize therefore the trajectory they were headed in, and then work to continue to move in that same direction.

Again, as a case in point, if the Bible is read as representing an ultimate ethic frozen in time, then the New Testament's witness to slavery, read in this way, would lead us to conclude that we should accept the institution of slavery as God's will. It is only by learning to recognize the trajectory in which the text is moving—plotting the course that the New Testament is *pointing us towards*—that we can truly follow Jesus forward. The alternative is to read Scripture in such a way that we get stuck in a past that accepts slavery and violence as normal and inevitable parts of life, using the Bible to justify and perpetuate these institutions as being ordained and approved of by God.

Reading on a trajectory thus means recognizing that what we find in the New Testament is not a final unchangeable eternal ethic, but rather the *first major concrete steps* away from the dominant religious and political narrative which understood oppression and violence as virtuous, and towards a better way rooted in compassion.

In the particular case of slavery, this entailed those in later times continuing to advance forward towards the abolition of the institution of slavery. The question for us in our time is how we can recognize the redemptive trajectory of the New Testament in other areas as well, allowing us to be on the cutting-edge of working towards a more compassionate and less violent world—plotting a course that leads us away from justifying violence and oppression, and instead towards compassion, grace, and enemy love.

A trajectory reading results in a forward-moving, growing, progressing ethic at the cutting-edge of moral advance, rather than one that is tethered to the past, often found on the side of fighting *against* moral progress in human and civil rights, being the very last to change, pulled kicking and screaming and dragging its feet into the future.

There are indeed enduring eternal principles found in Scripture, such as love, grace, and compassion. However we do not maintain those by standing still, but by ever seeking to grow and advance in them.

Jesus surely rejoiced when Martin Luther King demonstrated that nonviolence was applicable on a far larger scale than was seen at the time of Jesus, or when organizations like *Bread for the World* and *Compassion International* care for the poor in ways that far surpass what was possible back then through advances in transportation, education, nutrition, medicine, and so on. Jesus would have rejoiced to see this, because a good teacher always rejoices to see their students going beyond where they have gone. Jesus says this himself, "Very truly I tell you, whoever believes in me will do the works I have been doing, and *they will do even greater things than these*" (John 14:12, emphasis added).

WE ARE NOT SAFE

One objection to a trajectory reading is that it involves risk. What if we evaluate the trajectory incorrectly and head in the wrong direction? In contrast, the flat and frozen way of reading Scripture often presents itself as the only "safe" way to interpret the Bible. Listen to these words from John Henry Hopkins writing in the 19th century,

> If it were a matter to be determined by personal sympathies, tastes, or feelings, I should be as ready as any man to condemn the institution of slavery, for all prejudices of eduction, habit, and social position stand entirely opposed to it. But as a Christian... I am compelled to submit my weak and erring intellect to the authority of the Almighty. *For then only can I be safe in my conclusions.*[56]

The assumption here is that the "safe" way to read the Bible is to disregard our moral conscience, our compassion, our sense of right and wrong, ignoring everything we know about human

---

56 John Henry Hopkins (1792–1868) as cited in William Webb, *Moving Beyond the Bible to Theology* (Grand Rapids, Zondervan, 2009), 216. Emphasis added.

psychology and mental health, and instead blindly follow a text or law. This leads Hopkins to support the institution of slavery.

In reality, however, as Hopkins' example sadly illustrates, a reading devoid of conscience is anything but safe. It is precisely this kind of "safe" way of reading the Bible that has led people throughout history to commit unspeakable acts of cruelty and violence in the name of God. The problem is therefore not so much with the content of the Bible itself as it is learning to break away from a fundamentalist reading that leads to shutting down our conscience and justifying harm in God's name.

Today in our culture we regard slavery as self-evidently immoral. However, because their approach to the Bible itself has not changed, this leads many conservative Christians to continue to apply the same "safe" reading, promoting violence in other areas. Consider the following words by a contemporary Christian author (writing in 2005) promoting the corporal punishment of children, noting how similar the argument sounds to the one above by Hopkins:

> I would have never spanked them had I not been persuaded by the Word of God that God called me to this task. It is not my personality. Margy and I were exposed to some teaching from the book of Proverbs that convinced us that spanking had a valid place in parenting. We became persuaded that failure to spank would be unfaithfulness to their souls.[57]

---

57   Tedd Tripp, *Shepherding a Child's Heart*, 2nd ed. (Wapwallopen, PA: Shepherd, 2005), 109.

Again, we have someone going against their conscience, doing something they personally feel is wrong because they think this is what God demands of them, and moreover writing a book urging other parents to do the same—to go against their consciences, against their own parental sense of compassion, because the Bible supposedly tells them to. "You have no choice." He writes, "You are acting in obedience to God. It is your duty."[58]

At issue here is not so much the relative merit of the exact parental advice given by this author (which I happen to strongly disagree with), but far more importantly his claim that as Christians we are obligated as parents to blindly obey these directives, rather than working through these issues thoughtfully while listening to our conscience.

Parenting is a tremendous responsibility, and so it is vital to pay attention to our doubts and our conscience as we work through what is best for our kids. To instead say that parents are duty-bound to God to ignore their conscience, ignore their sense of compassion, as well as explicitly instructing his readers to ignore their pediatricians' advice, is a staggering recipe for disaster.[59]

Because the approach to interpretation has not changed, the argument made here by this author in the 21st century is an

---

58   Tripp, *Shepherding*, 32.

59   Tripp explicitly counsels parents to follow his "biblical" view even against the explicit advice of their pediatrician: "Therefore, formative instruction must be rooted in Scripture, *not in what ... the pediatrician tells us to do.*" Tedd and Margy Tripp, *Instructing a Child's Heart* (Wapwallopen, PA: Shepherd, 2008), 1. Emphasis added.

exact parallel to that made by Hopkins in the 19th century. Echoing Hopkins, almost word for word, he writes, "Experience is an unsafe guide. *The only safe guide is the Bible.*"[60]

The tragic reality however is that abrogating our moral responsibility as parents is anything but safe. This so-called "safe" way of reading against our conscience and better judgment has a long history of promoting violence as good. Consider the following sermon by John Wesley, the founder of the Methodist church, who counsels the use of physical violence to "break the wills" of children:

> This, therefore, I cannot but earnestly repeat—break their wills betimes; begin this great work before they can run alone, before they can speak plain, or perhaps speak at all. Whatever pains it cost, conquer their stubbornness: break the will, if you would not damn the child. I conjure you not to neglect, not to delay this! Therefore, (1.) Let a child, from a year old, be taught to fear the rod and to cry softly. In order to this, (2.) Let him have nothing he cries for; absolutely nothing, great or small; else you undo your own work. (3.) At all events, from that age, make him do as he is bid, if you whip him ten times running to effect it. Let none persuade you it is cruelty to do this; it is cruelty not to do it. Break his will now, and his soul will live, and he will probably bless you to all eternity.[61]

---

60 Tripp, *Shepherding*, introduction. Emphasis added.

61 John Wesley, "On Obedience to Parents," Sermon 96.

"Let none persuade you it is cruelty to do this" Those are surely haunting words. Moving from the 19th to the 20th century, we come to the words of the mother of the famous evangelist Billy Graham. Writing in 1977, she describes the regular occurrence in their home of her holding back tears as she stood by and watched her husband severely beat the young Billy with his belt:

> At such times I had to remind myself of another proverb, "withhold not correction from the child: for if thou beatest him with the rod, he will not die" (Proverbs 23:13). More than once I wiped tears away from my eyes and turned my head so the children wouldn't see. But I always stood by my husband when he administered discipline. I knew he was doing what was biblically correct. And the children didn't die.[62]

This is the bitter fruit of reading the Bible against one's conscience. It leads a mother to "turn her head" in the face of her child being beaten with a belt, passively accepting it as God's will, despite what her tears were trying to tell her. It lead John Wesley—who was himself abused by his puritan mother—to perpetuate that cycle of abuse, giving theological legitimacy to parents hardening their hearts and breaking their children's spirits. It has led countless people in the past to justify the brutal and inhumane institution of slavery, and it continues today to

---

62 Morrow C. Graham, quoted in Philip J. Greven, Jr., *Spare the Child: The Religious Roots of Punishment and the Psychological Impact of Physical Abuse* (New York: Knopf, 1991), 3.

lead many conservative Evangelicals to be some of the most outspoken advocates, not only of corporal punishment of children, but equally of gender inequality, discrimination against sexual minorities, torture, capital punishment, and of course war —all in a tragically misguided attempt to be "faithful" to the Bible.

We need to be clear here that Mrs. Graham is not describing a smack on the butt, but rather a severe beating that leaves wounds, which was sadly characteristic of parenting in past generations. She is correct that this is what is being advocated in the so-called "biblical model" found in the book of Proverbs and elsewhere in the Old Testament.

As William Webb has outlined in his study of corporal punishment and the Bible, while many contemporary advocates of "biblical" corporal punishment advocate spanking on the buttocks with an open hand, the Old Testament instead calls for striking a child with a whip or rod on the back or sides.[63]

Because this is where the internal organs are located, this not only leads to welts and bruises, but is also likely to cause internal bleeding. While leaving such marks on a child's body would be legal grounds for charges of child abuse today, such wounds are praised as a mark of virtue in Proverbs: "Blows and wounds scrub away evil, and beatings purge the inmost being" (Prov 23:30).

---

63 Webb, *Corporal Punishment*, 35–37.

Blows and wounds. This kind of physical abuse was sadly common practice in the past, including in New Testament times. Encouraging Christians who were enduring hardship and suffering, the author of the book of Hebrews quotes the book of Proverbs,

> My son, do not make light of the Lord's discipline, and do not lose heart when he rebukes you,
> because the Lord disciplines the one he loves, and he chastens everyone he accepts as his son. (Heb 12:5–6, quoting Prov 3:11–12 from the LXX)

The Greek word translated above in the NIV as "chastens" is *mastigoō* which in fact means "to beat with a whip, flog, scourge." Because we now view beating children with a whip as abuse, this has been softened in contemporary translations, but at the time scourging children was common practice. As the writer of Hebrews comments on the above verse, "What children are not disciplined by their father?" (v. 7).

If we read the Bible as a static record of God's unchanging principles, we would need to read this as a biblical endorsement of what we would today clearly regard as criminal child abuse. However, if we instead approach this from the perspective of a trajectory reading, we can recognize that this is simply a reflection of the reality of the time.

For the author and his original audience this was a "normal" and unquestioned part of their reality. This was a world where

135

people commonly beat their slaves and their children. Completely oblivious to it being problematic at all, it is given here as a comparative example his audience could all relate to in order to encourage them as they endured persecution.

This practice of beating children bloody continued for centuries, and only recently in modern times has this changed as we have increasingly come to realize the damage caused by abuse.

The simple fact is, if anyone were to apply the actual "biblical model" today found in the book of Proverbs and elsewhere in the Old Testament they would face criminal prosecution for child abuse. Thankfully, most advocates of corporal punishment today do not actually advocate the "biblical model" they claim to be upholding. As Webb points out, they have (unintentionally) progressed away from this model which would clearly be regarded as abusive today, and instead advocate a milder form of corporal punishment that does not leave physical wounds.

While this can be considered in some senses a positive improvement from the past, the trouble is, their milder version of corporal punishment is still radically out of step with *current* medicine and mental health. The American Academy of Pediatrics for example issued an official policy statement over a decade ago declaring that corporal punishment of children— including spanking—has potentially harmful side effects, and recommended that "parents be encouraged and assisted in the development of methods other than spanking for managing

136

undesired behavior."[64] Since then, further research has only strengthened these findings.

Webb thus encourages Christian advocates of corporal punishment to face up to the fact that they are not really following a "biblical" model at all (thank God), and to recognize that they have in fact moved forward in a redemptive direction towards more humane parenting. He appeals to them therefore to continue in the redemptive trajectory that they are already (accidentally) on—a trajectory that he argues is set by Scripture itself—taking it further by renouncing corporal punishment altogether.

READING ON MERIT

As we've seen, the unquestioning and authoritarian way of reading the Bible is anything but safe. In fact, it's profoundly dangerous and harmful. We need to instead plot out the trajectory of where Jesus' life-giving and counter-cultural message of grace and enemy love can take us, working to practically apply this to increasingly reducing violence and oppression in every area of our lives and world.

---

64 American Academy of Pediatrics, Committee on Psychosocial Aspects of Child and Family Health "Guidance for Effective Discipline," *Pediatrics* Vol. 101 No. 4 (April 1, 1998), 723–728. This statement was reaffirmed by the AAP in 2004.

This raises an important question: How do we identify the direction Jesus is going? How do we know what to embrace, and what to reject? How do we know for example that we should go beyond where the Bible did and abolish slavery, rather than upholding it? Are we simply following the accepted norms of our culture in regards to slavery today? To take another example, how do we know to embrace compassion and reject violence?

If there were universal agreement on these matters, this might be a moot point, however there are Christians today who seek to use the Bible to endorse violence as the vehicle of justice, and who conversely dismiss compassion as weak sentimentality. So how are we to determine in the final analysis who is right and who is wrong?

While it may seem obvious to us that we should focus on grace and love, there has been a long line of preachers over the centuries who have focused their message on fear and threat. On what basis can we say that they are wrong? How do we identify the trajectory Jesus and the New Testament is moving in, and differentiate this from the places where their thinking was still bound to the fallen and harmful views of their culture which regarded such things as slavery and child abuse as normal?

Our initial tendency is to try to find the "right" way to read a passage. So we ask: What is the *right* interpretation? The problem with this approach is that we quickly find that there are a host of conflicting voices—each claiming that *their* interpretation is the correct one. While the vast majority of biblical scholars would agree that reading the New Testament as endorsing violence entails a profound *misreading* of the text, there are still plenty of others who would disagree—and who could cite plenty of biblical texts to back up their view.

So again, how do we determine who is right? Are we dependent on scholars and experts to tell us the right interpretation? And if so, which expert, which authority, should we listen to and trust? Just as there are multiple competing narratives within the Old Testament, there are certainly multiple competing *interpretations* of the New Testament, each claiming to be the right one. How do we decide which interpretation is right?

Some have proposed here that we should look to the "historical Jesus" for our answers. This seems promising at first, but once again, we quickly find ourselves in the same place—with multiple conflicting hypothetical reconstructions of who exactly the "historical" Jesus was, each claiming to give us the "authentic" picture.

In the end, isn't this once again ultimately an authority-based argument that leaves us dependent on the authority of some biblical scholar or historian? Even if we were to do this, which authority would we pick? In a sea of differing interpretations—all claiming to be the real, authentic, and right one—how can we evaluate what to follow and further develop, and what to criticize and reject?

Many have suggested that we need to focus on Jesus. It has become increasingly popular for example to propose that we should read the Bible through a "Jesus-shaped" lens. This Jesus-shaped focus (or *Christocentric* focus, as it is often called) has been proposed by many as the key interpretive lens through which we must read all of Scripture—especially when dealing with troubling texts and countering a biblicist mindset.[65]

It's an attractive proposal, but we quickly encounter a number of difficulties with it, similar to those discussed above. First and foremost, this begs the question: *Which* interpretation of Jesus? There are of course those who seek to use Jesus to promote violent authoritarian readings of Scripture. How do we know that their reading is wrong, and one focused instead on compassion and enemy love is right? Further, how would this Jesus-lens work with difficulties in the New Testament itself such as the issue of slavery?

In order for a Jesus-lens to be practical we need to dig deeper to uncover the underlying hermeneutical lens that Jesus himself used as he read Scripture, and learn to apply this ourselves as we read. As we have seen, a central aspect of that is recognizing the difference between the way of *unquestioning obedience* that characterized how the Pharisees interpreted Scripture, and Jesus'

---

65 Some recent authors who have advocated such a Christocentric hermeneutic include Christian Smith, *The Bible Made Impossible*, 93–126; Eric A. Seibert, *Disturbing Divine Behavior: Troubling Old Testament Images of God* (Minneapolis: Fortress, 2009), 183–207; Peter Enns, *Inspiration and Incarnation: Evangelicals and the Problem of the Old Testament* (Grand Rapids: Baker Academic, 2005), 152–173. Michael Gorman has similarly focused on adopting Paul's *cruciform* spirituality which calls us to an understanding of the cross that is embodied in a Jesus-shaped life, Michael J. Gorman, *Cruciformity: Paul's Narrative Spirituality of the Cross* (Grand Rapids: Eerdmans, 2001) and *Inhabiting the Cruciform God: Kenosis, Justification, and Theosis in Paul's Narrative Soteriology* (Grand Rapids: Eerdmans, 2009).

way of *faithful questioning* which focused on love as the aim of Scripture.

What this looks like in practice is not an argument based on authority at all. As long as we are basing something on authority, we are not really understanding it. This is the way of *unquestioning obedience* which inevitably leads to hurtful interpretations because it has no means to differentiate between what is hurtful and what is loving.

If we truly wish to read the Bible in the way Jesus did, then this means that *we need to evaluate everything based on its merit*. If something is good, then we should be able to demonstrate its goodness in practice. This is the method Jesus himself proposed when he told us that we could spot a false prophet by looking at their fruits (Matt 7:16). *By their fruits you will recognize them*—that is the evaluative criterion Jesus gives us to use.

That's what having the "mind of Christ" is all about. When we do this, as Paul declares, we who are in Christ are *precisely* qualified to "judge all things" (1 Cor 2:15), and that includes lovingly confronting the ways that people (including ourselves) can interpret and apply Scripture in hurtful ways. Jesus is calling us, as his disciples, to a mature, intelligent, responsible and empowered reading of Scripture that is rooted in life and our shared human experience together.

Our hermeneutical key then is that our interpretation needs to be evaluated on its merit—we need to look at the fruits. If we see that it results in love then this is the aim of Scripture. If it instead results in harm then we are getting it wrong. With this simple evaluative criterion it becomes quite clear that interpreting the New Testament in order to justify the way of retribution, violent punishment, and subjugation has borne some pretty rotten fruit over the centuries.

In contrast, we can see the very real and demonstrable good that compassion, empathy, and restorative justice are doing in our world. We can taste and see that the way of grace, compassion, and enemy love is life-giving and good, and likewise we can equally observe the many ways that fear and violence are deeply harmful. To put it bluntly: Grace is amazing, and genocide, slavery and child abuse are not.

The true test for what we should embrace or reject in the Bible is therefore demonstrated *in practice*—borne out in the fruits of our lives and relationships. We look at the fruits, and judge whether they are sweet or rotten. We evaluate a claim in the Bible the same way we evaluate any claim—based on its merit. This is not a matter of subjective opinion, but of observing the evidence (the fruits) in real life.

It is not an "opinion," for instance, that hand washing is connected to preventing the spread of germs. This is simply an undeniable fact of life based on observable evidence. Similarly, because of human psychology we now understand the devastating harm that comes from child abuse.

In biblical times, because the natural and social sciences did not yet exist, they had no such understanding, and thus child abuse was the norm (indeed, the concept of child abuse itself did not exist). Again, our modern realization that child abuse is profoundly damaging is not merely a subjective "opinion," it is an undeniable conclusion based on observable evidence.

We therefore can evaluate a biblical claim by its fruits, by the evidence of its observable effects in people's lives—evaluating whether it results in flourishing or harm, peace or devastation. We look at the fruits in life and observe if they are sweet or rotten. This is our evaluative benchmark.

Because we know based on observable evidence that child abuse and slavery are deeply harmful, this leads us to re-assess how we have understood God to be endorsing them in Scripture, just as the discovery that the earth revolved around the sun has caused the church to re-assess its geocentric model of the universe.

This does not necessarily mean that the Bible is wrong on these points. It could very well be that we have misread the Bible, and need to dig deeper to uncover what is really being said. For example, one could argue that the geocentric view found in Scripture is better understood as a pre-scientific phenomenological perspective that is misunderstood when taken as a scientific description.

Be that as it may, the bottom line is that our interpretation of Scripture needs to coincide with actual reality, and this is most important where it affects ethics. We cannot afford to shut down our mind and conscience as we read. On the contrary, a moral

143

reading of Scripture requires that we fully engage both our mind and conscience. If we therefore recognize that a particular interpretation leads to observable harm, this necessarily means that we need to stop and reassess our course. To continue on a course we know to be harmful, simply because "the Bible says so," is morally irresponsible.

PRIORITIZING CARE

It is worth noting the difference between Webb's approach to a trajectory reading, and the one I have outlined above. While we both share the same hermeneutical approach of recognizing the trajectory set by Jesus and continuing in that same direction, we differ somewhat in how to determine the direction of that trajectory.

As outlined above, my focus is on Jesus' evaluative criterion of "looking at the fruits" observable in life. While Webb similarly allows for the inclusion of such social-scientific evidence, his primary focus is on a comparison between the cultural norms of the biblical authors vis-a-vis the values of the surrounding cultures.

This leads Webb to conclude that homosexuality is wrong because he does not see any signs of ancient Hebrew culture being more open towards it than the surrounding cultures, and in fact observes that the opposite is the case.

In contrast, I would argue that it would be more important to observe the effects that same-sex relationships have in life today, than it would be to ask what the respective views of past cultures may have been. Do we find evidence that same-sex relationships lead to harm or that they lead to flourishing? The overwhelming majority of social scientists and mental health practitioners today would maintain that there is simply no evidence that same-sex relationships are destructive or harmful in and of themselves.[66]

Conversely, what we can observe, as far as harm is concerned, is that statistically the LGBT community has a higher rate of drug abuse, mental illness, and suicide than the larger population —alarmingly higher in fact.[67] The reason is quite clear: the rejection they experience.

Being kicked out of their homes, hiding who they are, being threatened and hated, etc. can easily make a person sick, depressed, broken, and even drive them to suicide. As their voices have begun to be heard, we have seen story after story of how

---

66 While Webb and I differ here, I want to stress that we have much more we agree on. So while we are at different places now, we are all growing and learning, and I hope my above criticism is heard in the spirit of dialog reflecting the very real respect and appreciation I have for him and the important work he is doing.

67 For a good overview of the research on this topic, as well as recommendation for prevention, see the following study prepared for the U.S. Department of Health and Human Services by the Suicide Prevention Resource Center. "Suicide risk and prevention for lesbian, gay, bisexual, and transgender youth" (Newton, MA: Education Development Center, Inc., 2008) available online at http://www.sprc.org/library/SPRC_LGBT_Youth.pdf

gay and transgender kids have felt hated, at times even hating themselves.

That really should be a wakeup call for us. While there is no evidence that same-sex relationships are themselves harmful, there is a considerable amount of evidence that the condemnation and rejection the LGBT community faces is profoundly harmful.

Regardless of whether we believe homosexuality is right or wrong, none of that matters much when people are dying. If we truly care about people, then the practical question straight Christians need to be asking is: Are we helping or hurting with the way we are responding to gays? Are we promoting grace or promoting harm? If it turns out that a moral stance in opposition to homosexuality is having the unintended affect of fueling this kind of rejection, leading to self-hatred and even suicide among gays, then we need to seriously re-think our priorities and focus.

We can of course argue over what the Bible says about homosexuality, but one thing is utterly clear: Jesus teaches us to love people, not to hate them, not to make them feel hated, and not to stand by while that is happening. From the perspective of the New Testament there simply is no room for doubt on this. We know exactly where Jesus stands in this regard. He stands on the side of the least, the condemned, the vulnerable.

Looking at Jesus, we can clearly observe in the Gospels that his priority was on caring for the welfare of *people*, in contrast to the Pharisees who instead prioritized the maintenance of their moral standards. We need to get our priorities straight and prioritize compassion in our witness towards gays—even if that means, like Jesus, having the reputation among the Pharisees of today of being a "friend of sinners."

Again, as stated above, if we recognize that our particular interpretation and application of Scripture is leading to observable harm, this necessarily means that we need to stop and reassess our course. Scripture, as Jesus read it, needs to lead us to love God, others, and ourselves. If we find that it is leading instead to causing harm then we are getting it wrong.

NOT SAFE, BUT GOOD

Becoming thinking and morally responsible readers is hard work. It certainly would be easier if we could just flip open to a certain page and find the right answer in our Bibles. But, unless we want to endorse slavery and child abuse today, we need to face the fact that the New Testament is simply not that kind of book. What we find instead is a radical and life-giving message of grace and enemy love that still remains surprising, subversive, and counter-cultural some 2000 years later.

We don't find this way of enemy love expressed in its final form however, but instead see it emerging out of the messy reality of life at the time—marking the first crucial steps on an upwards trajectory out of the dead-end way of retribution and

147

fear, and charting an alternate course in the direction of grace, compassion, and enemy love. Being faithful to that way means learning to recognize and cultivate what is good, inspiring, and challenging in Scripture, and then continuing to move further in that same redemptive direction today.

In this chapter we've seen a trajectory approach to Scripture that works hand in hand with the sciences, allowing us to read Scripture in such a way that it leads us to love, evaluating this by observing the effects it has in our lives. Just as the sciences are always growing and progressing in knowledge, this approach to Scripture allows for an approach to morality that is likewise always growing and progressing—moving towards an ever more sophisticated application of the way of restorative justice, compassion, and enemy love, finding practical ways to apply this to the many needs and problems in our complex world. In the end, it comes down to reading the Bible like grown-ups—fully engaging our intelligence and approaching the text as morally responsible readers. That may not be "safe" or easy, but it is most certainly good.

CHAPTER 7

GOD AND THE STATE SWORD

While the New Testament itself is focused on peace and nonviolence, it is at the same time an undeniable historical fact that the New Testament has been (mis)used to promote violence and oppression—not only in the past but today as well. While the majority of New Testament scholars would regard endorsements of human violence in God's name as a grave misreading of the New Testament, there are nevertheless some who continue to try to justify state sanctioned violence in the name of Jesus. In this chapter, we will explore several of these misguided arguments, which have tragically been used to justify policies of torture, beatings, and death.

WAR IMAGERY: In some cases the arguments used by those who wish to use the New Testament to justify violence are quite transparent and can be uncovered with a simple appeal to genre and context. For example, some have sought to appeal to violent war imagery, such as when Paul speaks of "putting on the full armor of God" in Ephesians 6 as an endorsement of polices of institutional violence.

Of course this reading overlooks the entire point of the passage which is to ready ourselves for the "gospel of peace" (v. 15). Paul also makes clear that "our struggle is not against flesh and blood," that is, we don't fight people, we fight the evil in all of us by the means of doing good. The New Testament does use violent imagery, because it is written in a time where that imagery was a part of their every day experience.

However, in using this imagery, the New Testament consistently subverts the ethos of violence, reshaping it into a vision of overcoming evil with goodness and love. In other words, this is an example of protest-narrative arising out of a culture where war is considered to be glorious (as it continues to be presented in the vast majority of American action movies today).

This vocabulary is subverted and instead used to promote the way of peace, and to stress that our "fight" is not against people at all, but against hate, against violence. Paul is flipping the script.

THE FAITH OF THE CENTURION: Another appeal made by advocates of violence is to cite Jesus' praise of a Roman centurion as implying his endorsement of the military. However, a closer examination reveals that this is in fact an illustration of enemy love.

Jesus holds up the faith of this pagan soldier, who embodied for his fellow Jews an enemy oppressor, and provocatively declares, "I tell you, I have not found such great faith even in Israel" (Luke 7:9). In a similar declaration, Jesus says, "Truly I tell you, the tax collectors and the prostitutes are entering the kingdom of God ahead of you" (Matt 21:31). In both of these examples, those who are normally viewed with contempt are set forth here by Jesus as examples of faithfulness, turning the tables on the prejudices of his religious audience.

This is enemy love in action. To instead read Jesus' first statement as an endorsement of the military is just as inappropriate as reading his second statement as an endorsement of prostitution. What both of these examples do illustrate is that Jesus does not turn away anyone, regardless of how despised they may have been in the people's eyes.

Again, this is an example of a protest-narrative which challenges the religious and cultural assumptions of its audience which placed people in an us/them dynamic. Jesus is breaking

151

those boundaries by showing the virtue and faith of one who would have been commonly regarded as an enemy oppressor. To instead read this as an endorsement of war is therefore to completely miss the point.

JESUS AND BUYING SWORDS: An often cited example employed by those seeking to justify violence with the New Testament is Jesus' statement to his disciples, "if you don't have a sword, sell your cloak and buy one" (Luke 22:36). The disciples respond, "See, Lord, here are two swords" (v. 38).

The response of Jesus to his disciples is important: Many older translations render it as "That is enough" as if Jesus were making the absurd claim that two swords would be enough to take on Rome. However, as Joseph Fitzmyer notes in his commentary on Luke, a better reading of the Greek here would be a rebuke: "Enough of this!"[68]

This is echoed again at the end of this chapter when Jesus is arrested, and one of the disciples pulls out his sword and attacks the servant of the high priest, cutting off his ear. Jesus again rebukes them with the terse words "No more of this!" (v. 51) and then proceeds to heal the man's ear. Matthew's account records

---

68 Joseph Fitzmyer, *The Gospel According to Luke*, 2 vols. *Anchor Bible* 28 & 28a (Garden City, NY: Doubleday, 1985), 1428. This same reading has been adopted by new translations such as the NIV which adds an exclamation point to signify rebuke, "That's enough!" and the NET which notes here that "The disciples' misunderstanding caused Jesus to terminate the discussion." Yoder suggests that Jesus is quoting the LXX of Deuteronomy 3:26 "*That is enough!* the LORD said. Do not speak to me anymore about this matter!" John Howard Yoder, *The Politics of Jesus* (Grand Rapids: Eerdmans, 1994), 45, n. 44.

Jesus as declaring here, "Put your sword back in its place, for all who draw the sword will die by the sword!" (Matt 26:52).

So why did Jesus tell his disciples to buy swords in the first place if he did not want them to use them? A number of explanations have been offered by various scholars. Some suggest that it was in order to fulfill the prophecy which Jesus then immediately quotes following this statement, "If you don't have a sword, sell your cloak and buy one. It is written: 'And he was numbered with the transgressors'; and I tell you that this must be fulfilled in me. Yes, what is written about me is reaching its fulfillment" (Luke 22:36–37).

Note that Jesus is quoting here from Isaiah 53. In seeing the prophecy of the suffering servant of Isaiah 53 as being fulfilled in himself, Jesus demonstrates an understanding the role of messiah as one who bears unjust suffering and violence, and decidedly *not* of a militant warrior messiah who needs swords. Thus when Luke records the arrest of Jesus in this same chapter, we read Jesus declaring, "Am I leading a rebellion, that you have come with swords and clubs?" (Luke 22:52).

Whatever the intent of Jesus in telling his disciples to buy a sword, one thing becomes abundantly clear from everything else that happens surrounding this statement: *Jesus did not intend to have his disciples use them.* Jesus clearly rebukes them for this, heals the injured man, and issues several statements categorically rejecting the use of the sword.

From this it becomes clear that this is one of the many examples found throughout the Gospels of Jesus' disciples misunderstanding his intentions and way. Jesus was making a symbolic prophetic utterance, and when his disciples took his statement to "buy a sword" literally, he rebuked them for missing the point. Apparently, that misunderstanding still persists today among some of his modern-day disciples.

NOT PEACE, BUT A SWORD: A similar example is Jesus' declaration, "I have not come to bring peace, but a sword" (Matt 10:34). Taken out of context, this may appear to be an endorsement of the use of violence; however, when we look closer, we can again see that this is clearly not the case.

Looking at the parallel account in Luke, we see that the "sword" mentioned in Matthew is metaphorical, referring to division: "Do you think I came to bring peace on earth? No, I tell you, but *division*" (Luke 12:51). The practice of enemy love can indeed cause division: Expanding the definition of who we include in "us" to include the outsider and even the enemy can often be perceived as an act of disloyalty by our own group, family, or nation. We can see in the Gospels many examples of how Jesus experienced such hostility as he reached out to those considered enemies and outsiders.

Again, Jesus is describing here the conflict that results when we break out of the normal us/them boundaries of family and tribe, provocatively describing the conflict that comes when we stand up for the marginalized and the other in the name of love.

THE TEMPLE INCIDENT: Jesus overturning the money-changer's tables, and driving out the animals with a whip is often cited by those who wish to legitimize violence. The incident is recorded in all of the synoptic Gospels (Matt 21:12–17; Mark 11:15–19; Luke 19:45–48), but the most detailed account is found in John:

> In the temple courts he found people selling cattle, sheep and doves, and others sitting at tables exchanging money. So he made a whip out of cords, and drove all from the temple courts, both sheep and cattle; he scattered the coins of the money changers and overturned their tables. To those who sold doves he said, "Get these out of here! Stop turning my Father's house into a market!" (John 2:14–16, NRSV).

The first thing we need to notice here is that people are not being driven out with his makeshift whip, cows and sheep are.[69] Jesus does not physically harm anyone. He does of course upset a lot of people, but he did that frequently.

This is an example of what Ched Myers aptly describes as a symbolic public enactment in line with the prophetic tradition.[70]

---

69 See John Howard Yoder, *The Politics of Jesus* (Grand Rapids: Eerdmans, 1994), 42–43; William M. Swartley, *Covenant of Peace: The Missing Peace in New Testament Theology and Ethics* (Grand Rapids: Eerdmans, 2006), 112.

70 Ched Myers, *Binding the Strongman: A Political Reading of Mark's Story of Jesus* (Maryknoll, NY: Orbis, 1988).

Jesus is not losing his cool, he is enacting a symbolic public protest against the corruption of the temple system. As Richard Hays comments, "It is an act of violence in approximately the same way that anti-nuclear protestors commit an act of violence when they break into a Navy base and pour blood on nuclear submarines."[71]

If anything can be taken as normative here from Jesus' actions, it would be his modeling of civil disobedience and public protest in defiance of the existing religious authorities. In no way can it be seen as a justification for harming others—whether that is in the name of the state, or in the name of rebellion against the state. Jesus categorically rejected the way of violence as a means for advancing God's kingdom and way, and this is no exception.

Richard Hays concludes that "from Matthew to Revelation we find a consistent witness against violence and a calling to the community to follow the example of Jesus in *accepting* suffering rather than *inflicting* it ... Nowhere does the New Testament provide any positive model of Jesus or his followers employing violence in defense of justice."[72] The simple fact is that looking to Jesus for a legitimization of violence is grasping at straws. It can only be sustained when one begins with an external set of assumptions of how the world ought to function, and then

---

71 Richard Hays, *The Moral Vision of the New Testament: Community, Cross, New Creation, A Contemporary Introduction to New Testament Ethics* (San Francisco: HarperSanFrancisco, 1996), 334.

72 Hays, *Moral Vision*, 332, 340. Emphasis in original.

156

attempts to artificially project these assumptions onto the New Testament.

Of all the many ways people can misread the New Testament, the attempt to warp Jesus into an advocate for authoritarian violence is by far the most implausible and absurd. Perhaps the most revealing and sad contemporary example of this is that of the hyper-Calvinist preacher Mark Driscoll, who writes:

> In Revelation, Jesus is a prize-fighter with a tattoo down his leg, a sword in his hand and the commitment to make someone bleed. That is the guy I can worship. I cannot worship the hippie, diaper, halo Christ because I cannot worship a guy I can beat up.[73]

What's so revealing about Driscoll's statement is that it strips away the polite veneer that is so often present when theologians attempt to justify violence in dignified and noble sounding terms. Giving new meaning to the term "bully pulpit," Driscoll in his troubling immaturity inadvertently confronts us with the ugliness and brutality of this violent theology in all of its absurdity. There simply are no grounds for using the New Testament to justify human violence. The only way to argue otherwise is to project our own violence onto Jesus, resulting in the sad picture above.

---

73 Mark Driscoll, "7 Big Questions" *Relevant Magazine* #24 (Jan/Feb 2007). http://web.archive.org/web/20071013102203/http://relevantmagazine.com/god_article.php?id=7418

PAUL AND THE STATE SWORD

While advocates of religiously justified violence will reference the occasional out of context statement of Jesus as we have seen in many of the above examples, a favorite point of reference for justifying state violence in God's name is the apostle Paul, and in particular Romans 13. In this chapter Paul declares that "rulers do not bear the sword for no reason. They are God's servants, agents of wrath to bring punishment on the wrongdoer" (v. 4). Proponents of violence are quick to seize this as a biblical mandate for the state's use of violent punishment, including the death penalty.

Paul's statement here must be understood in its fuller context of Romans 12–13. In the chapter immediately preceding this one (Romans 12), Paul has just finished admonishing the church in Rome not to take revenge or seek payback, but instead to take up the way of enemy love. So it seems odd that he would then abruptly reverse himself in the next chapter, suddenly arguing in favor of the retributive justice he had just rejected. So in order to better understand what Paul was saying in context, we'll need to begin by taking a look at Romans 12, before addressing Paul's statements in Romans 13.

ROMANS 12 AND ENEMY LOVE: Paul begins this chapter with an appeal for us to imitate the way of Christ:

Therefore, I urge you, brothers and sisters, in view of God's mercy, to offer your bodies as a living sacrifice, holy and pleasing to God—this is your true and proper worship. Do not conform to the pattern of this world, but be transformed by the renewing of your mind. Then you will be able to test and approve what God's will is—his good, pleasing and perfect will. (Rom 12:1–2)

Note here that Paul says our response to God's act of enemy love in Christ is to likewise become a "living sacrifice" by adopting a new way of thinking that does not conform "to the pattern of this world," but rather is characterized by a renewed imagination—a Jesus-shaped imagination. Paul tells us here that the way we can know God's "good, pleasing and perfect will" is by our having the way of Jesus change how we think, renewing our minds, and this subsequently "transforming" both us and our relationships.

Paul next outlines what that looks like in practice, echoing Jesus' Sermon on the Mount so closely that some scholars have wondered if Paul had a copy in hand when he wrote Romans:

Bless those who persecute you; bless and do not curse. Rejoice with those who rejoice; mourn with those who mourn. Live in harmony with one another. Do not be proud, but be willing to associate with people of low position. Do not be conceited.

Do not repay anyone evil for evil. Be careful to do what is right in the eyes of everyone. If it is possible, as far as it depends on you, live at peace with everyone. Do not take revenge, my dear friends, but leave room for God's wrath, for it is written: "It is mine to avenge; I will repay," says the Lord. On the contrary:

"If your enemy is hungry, feed him; if he is thirsty, give him something to drink. In doing this, you will heap burning coals on his head."

Do not be overcome by evil, but overcome evil with good. (Rom 12:14–21)

Paul quotes Deuteronomy 32 here, citing the prophetic declaration "It is mine to avenge" in order to argue that we should not seek vengeance, but rather work to "overcome evil with good" (v. 21). As we saw in chapter three, Paul frequently reversed the original meaning of Old Testament passages which endorsed violence. He is doing the same again here. The original passage reads as a celebration of violent payback:

It is mine to avenge; I will repay ... I will take vengeance on my adversaries and repay those who hate me. I will make my arrows drunk with blood, while my sword devours flesh: the blood of the slain and the captives, the heads of the enemy leaders. (Deut 32:35, 41–42)

Paul takes this passage, which originally advocated and glorified vengeance and violence in war, and instead now employs it to argue for the very opposite: "Do not take revenge" (v.19). Once again, Paul has reversed and subverted the meaning of this violent text.

ROMANS 13 AND INSURRECTION: Assuming that Paul has not suddenly decided in the very next chapter to endorse the way of retribution and repaying evil for evil that he just finished telling us not to follow, how are we to understand his statements here?

The standard answer by those who seek to use the New Testament to justify state violence and retributive justice is to claim that we as individuals should not practice retaliation, but that the state (and therefore anyone working for the state) is mandated by God to use violence in the name of justice.

By this logic, the way of Jesus only applies to private matters, and has no relevance for shaping the public sphere or our larger social interactions—including apparently what we do in the name of our so-called "Christian nation." In this view, vengeance and violence carried out by the state are viewed as expressions of "justice" sanctioned by God. The result has been a privatization of religion, giving kings and CEOs a sort of "diplomatic immunity" to the gospel.

Looking at the immediate context of Romans 13:1-7, however, we can see that Paul is not proposing a general theory of government which would blatantly contradict everything he has just said in Romans 12. Once again, this is the mistake of reading the Bible as if it were a static book of timeless principles divorced from any cultural context.

The reality is that this is a specific letter to the church in Rome where Paul is addressing a specific circumstance of this persecuted minority community in the midst of a violent and brutal regime, and suggesting how they should apply what he has just said about following the way of Christ within their particular context. In other words, Romans 13 is a practical application of the way of enemy love that Paul has just outlined in Romans 12, tailored to their specific situation.

That situation, New Testament scholar Willard Swartley suggests, was a brewing tax revolt in Rome under Nero.[74] Nero came into power in 54AD, and the Roman historian Tacitus tells of a growing tax revolt that Nero faced in the early years of emperorship. This would coincide with Paul's letter to the Romans, which he wrote from Corinth around 56–57AD.

This historical background lines up with what Paul writes in Romans 13, concluding his argument, "Therefore it is necessary to be in subjection, not only because of the wrath of the authorities but also because of your conscience. *For this reason you also pay taxes … Pay everyone what is owed: taxes to whom taxes are due, revenue to whom revenue is due*" (Rom 13:5–6, NET). Swartley argues that Paul's concern here with taxes is that if the church in Rome

---

74   See Willard M. Swartley, *Covenant of Peace: The Missing Peace in New Testament Theology and Ethics* (Downers Grove: Eerdmans, 2006), 239, footnote 34.

were to join in this revolt, this would be seen as an act of rebellion, and thus result in bringing down the wrath of Rome upon them, "Whoever rebels against the authority … will bring judgment on themselves" (v. 2).

PAUL'S HISTORICAL CONTEXT: To understand what a volatile issue this was, it is important to grasp the political situation that existed at the time under the Roman emperor Nero. Nero is the Roman emperor famous for blaming Christians for the fire in Rome, and using them as human torches in 64 AD. Roman senator and historian Tacitus describes the situation:

> Nero fastened the guilt and inflicted the most exquisite tortures on a class hated for their abominations, called Christians by the populace. Christus, from whom the name had its origin, suffered the extreme penalty during the reign of Tiberius at the hands of one of our procurators, Pontius Pilatus, … An immense multitude was convicted, not as much of the crime of firing the city as of hatred against mankind. Mockery of every sort was added to their deaths. Covered with the skins of beasts, they were torn by dogs and perished, or were nailed to crosses, or were doomed to the flames and burnt, to serve as a nightly illumination, when daylight had expired.[75]

---

75 Tacitus, *Annals* 15.44. Alfred John Church and William Jackson Brodribb (trans.), *The Complete Works of Tacitus* (New York: McGraw-Hill, 1964), 380–81.

Tacitus explains that Nero's violence was so perverse that even the Roman populace recognized the injustice of what was being done to the persecuted church, "There arose a feeling of compassion; for it was not, as it seemed, for the public good, but to glut one man's cruelty, that they were being destroyed."[76]

Here we see the character of the king in all his ugliness. This was the Rome Paul lived in under Nero. It is therefore rather implausible to read Paul's statement in Romans 13:1 that "the authorities that exist have been established by God" as a blanket approval for the justice of the state. Just as Nazi Germany stands as a clear example of an unjust state, so too did Nero's Rome. Similarly, just as Jews in Nazi Germany could recognize signs of Hitler's tyranny long before this erupted into the horror of the concentration camps, surely Paul was likewise not naive in regards to the character of Nero when he wrote his letter to the church in Rome just a few short years before the ghastly tale of human torches in 64 AD.

Jews like Paul at the time did not see the Roman occupation as just by any means, and the oppression and tyranny illustrated in the above incident was just another episode in a long line of suffering on the part of Jews (and Christians) under Rome.

Paul's statement here is thus echoing a common Jewish perspective as a marginalized people which insisted that human rulers were not sovereign, but only had their authority on loan from God. This same defiant notion is captured in the response

---

76   Ibid.

of Jesus to Pilate when he says to him "Don't you realize I have power either to free you or to crucify you?" Jesus answers, "You would have no power over me if it were not given to you from above. Therefore the one who handed me over to you is guilty of a greater sin" (John 19:10–11).

Note here that Jesus is accusing Pilate of sin. Likewise, Romans 13:1–7 must be understood in the context of the volatile relationship that the Jews—as well as the early church—had under the oppressive rule of Rome. Remember that Paul himself was charged with crimes by the state, beaten multiple times, jailed, and eventually executed by Rome. So to see Paul as a cheerleader for the goodness of the Roman imperial state under Nero is to miss the volatile and hostile historical reality of Paul's situation at the time.

We thus see in Romans 12–13 a snapshot of Paul's attempt to navigate the church in Rome through a volatile and dangerous relationship within a violent regime—modeling the way of enemy love, rather than the way of retaliation. Taking Romans 12 and 13 together, Paul's counsel to the church in Rome is: *Do not be conformed to the pattern of this world* (Rom 12:2), *but do not commit an act of open insurrection that will result in bringing down the crushing arm of the Roman state either.* In other words, Paul is telling the church in Rome to resist via the means of overcoming evil with good, not through the means of retaliation and insurrection —a way he knows will lead to mass bloodshed.

OUR HISTORICAL CONTEXT: Paul's context was a time when Christianity was a persecuted minority struggling under severe oppression and injustice. Paul therefore draws a sharp distinction between the way of the state and the way of Christ. Today our situation in the West is very different, and it is not uncommon for Christians to find themselves in the position of being able to influence and change society in significant ways. We therefore find ourselves in the position of being able to wrestle with a question Paul couldn't: *What does it look like to shape our society in the way of Jesus?*

If today we have the ability to shape how we as a society deal with crime or international conflict, or can positively affect policy for how the vulnerable are treated, should we refuse to do so, instead insisting that Christ's followers should not be involved in the state? Or if we do become involved, should we simply mirror the way of Rome, the way of retaliation? Isn't there perhaps a third option? Instead of extracting ourselves from the world or simply mirroring the state's way of violence, what if we used the influence we have to promote making our institutions more in-line with the values and way of Jesus?

As we've seen in the previous chapter, the New Testament's "on the page" approach to slavery calls for slaves to submit in the face of the oppression and abuse that characterized slavery at the time. Likewise, we have also seen here Paul arguing in Romans 13 for the persecuted church in Rome to submit to Nero's deeply unjust state sword. Many conservative Christians, reading the

Bible as a static depository of eternal truths, take Romans 13 as God's endorsement for the use of state violence today—just as Christians in the past took similar New Testament statements as a biblical endorsement of slavery in their day.

In fact, we see Peter making a very similar statement to Paul's in regard to submitting to the governing authorities, and in the same breath telling slaves to submit to their masters, "Be subject to every human institution for the Lord's sake, whether to a king as supreme or to governors as those he commissions to punish wrongdoers and praise those who do good. ... *Slaves, be subject to your masters with all reverence, not only to those who are good and gentle, but also to those who are perverse* (1 Peter 2:13–18).

A trajectory reading instead identifies the direction the New Testament is moving in its core narrative of enemy love, and recognizes that this should lead us today *away* from justifying state violence and retribution, just as it led us in the past away from justifying the institution of slavery. While counseling submission to the immoral institution of slavery and to the brutal regime of Nero's Rome may have been a needed survival strategy at a time when the church was a persecuted minority, this does not mean that we should continue to uphold the institution of slavery today, nor that we should have kings instead of democracy, *nor does it mean that we should continue to uphold state violence and the sword as God's will either.*

167

With slavery this is a rather easy conclusion to reach looking back from the vantage point of the 21st century where we all agree that slavery is obviously wrong. It was harder for American Christians to see this in the pre-Civil War era, living in a time where slavery was the norm.

For us today—living in a time when the primary way we think about crime is still in terms of retribution and punishment, and the primary way we think we are strong, safe, and bring about "justice" in the world is through military force—it is equally difficult for us to see how the way of Jesus understood on a trajectory might provide us with a more effective and more humane way of dealing with crime and international conflict than the way of Rome does. The challenge of our time therefore is to work towards the abolition of retribution.

Change in this direction is already taking place today. Not only have we abolished the institution of slavery, we have also established social systems to care for the poor, enacted multiple human rights laws, and passed laws outlawing corporal punishment. We need to continue in that same direction, working to reduce violence and promote God's restorative justice in our world.

These are values that can stand on their own merit on the world stage—values that can be demonstrated to be effective and good. Part of our task involves articulating these Jesus-shaped values in a practical and intelligible way, so it is clear not only why we as followers of Jesus should embrace them, but also clear why everyone should. With this in mind, the next chapter will look at the merits of enemy love understood as an alternative to the way of Rome and the state sword, outlining how it can be practically applied on both a personal and societal level.

CHAPTER 8

A PRACTICAL GUIDE TO ENEMY-LOVE

L et's take a moment to review where we've gotten to in the book thus far, and where we are headed. We began with the Old Testament and saw that it contains multiple conflicting narratives—some justifying violence, others protesting violence; some promoting mercy, others commanding "show them no mercy." How do we choose between these conflicting views? Learning to read the Bible like Jesus involves understanding what led him to embrace what he did in the multi-vocal Hebrew Bible and then adopting those same priorities as we read.

This Jesus-shaped reading of course brings us to the New Testament. While it can clearly be seen that radical forgiveness and enemy love are central to the message of Jesus and the New Testament, at the same time we have seen that, when read on a surface level, an "on the page" reading of the New Testament leads us to conclude that slavery and child abuse are ordained by God. The alternative is to instead adopt a trajectory reading that does not stop at "treat your slaves kindly," but recognizes that faithfulness to the way of Jesus requires that we go beyond where they were able to go at the time, and continues to move forward towards the abolition of slavery.

In the previous chapter we next looked at Paul's response to Rome's use of violence as a way of dealing with crime and international conflict, and proposed that while it was understandable that the church took the position of submission to the state at a time when it was a persecuted minority under the oppressive rule of Nero's Rome—just as it took a parallel position at the time in regards to slavery—this does not mean that we should limit the application of Christ's way of enemy love to the private sphere today when we have the possibility of shaping our society to reflect the values of Jesus, rather than simply mirroring the way of Rome.

Just as it was difficult to see that slavery was wrong in the past, it is difficult for us today to see that there are better ways to deal with crime and international conflict—not only because this conflicts with an "on the page" reading of the Bible, but also because it goes against the grain of our thinking as a society that still deeply trusts in violence—especially in our American society.

We can see this reflected in our national rhetoric, and we can see it reflected in our films and television shows which perpetually rehearse the necessity of violence as the means to bring about "justice" and ensure our safety. As a society we trust in violence. We think it keeps us safe; we think it makes us strong.

Given that, it will not be enough to simply note the harm that comes from violence. We will need to demonstrate to the world that there are viable nonviolent means of dealing with societal problems—ways that are not only effective, but in fact *more* effective than violence is at resolving conflict, and keeping us safe as a society.

Such a pursuit should not be seen as a detour in a book on reading the Bible. The central aim of Scripture, as Jesus saw it, was to lead us to love. Our reading of Scripture therefore is merely academic unless we can translate it into action.

If the core teaching of Jesus is rooted in enemy love, then a major role of the interpretive task is to work out how to apply this in our time. Outlining how Christ's way of enemy love might practically be applied as a real solution to our real world problems will therefore be the focus of this chapter.

173

BREAKING OUT OF THE
"WHAT IF..." TRAP

If you've ever been part of a discussion on nonviolence, you'll know that, more often than not, the conversation finds its way to the infamous "what if?" question, where an extreme no-win scenario is presented that goes something like this:

> *Hitler has broken into your house and is holding your wife at gun point, you happen to have a gun in your hand, too, and are good enough of a shot that you can take out Adolf without harming your wife, but not good enough of a shot that you could shoot the gun out of his hand. So do you stand by and do nothing, or do you shoot to kill?*

Such questions are really more of an accusation, asserting that it would be immoral not to protect our loved ones if they were in danger. It's a question asked in exasperation, "Of *course* you should shoot the bad guy and save your loved one!" they scream inwardly. To neglect this would be a scandal, it would be foolishness.

On the other side of the argument we have those who are seeking to be faithful to follow Jesus' command to love our enemies. Their desire is to end the vicious spirals of violence, but this *what-if* question backs them into the corner, portraying them as negligent in caring for their loved ones if they do not pull the trigger.

On both sides of this debate are people who deeply care about the welfare of others. On one side we see a desire to protect and defend, and on the other a concern to renounce the dead-end way of retribution and violence. What's so painfully frustrating is that framing the debate in this way polarizes both sides, effectively bringing constructive discussion to a standstill. It's a classic example of an "us vs. them" dynamic where each side regards the other as the bad guy.

Like a Chinese finger trap, the more you struggle, the more stuck you get—each side reacts, and the polarization just gets deeper and deeper. So how can we both break out? How can we respect the concerns of people on both sides of the debate, bringing us out of the deadlock and into a productive conversation? This is the essential question of nonviolence: How can we break out of the trap where each side sees the other as the "bad guy"?

For those of us on the side of nonviolence, we need to begin by acknowledging the legitimate concerns of those who argue in favor of violence. Their concern is to protect loved ones, and violence is the only means they can see to do this. When life is on the line this naturally triggers deep emotional reactions, it evokes our survival instincts, and consequently people may express themselves in rash ways at times, but at heart we need to recognize the legitimate and healthy concern for self-care behind people's objections to enemy love. Such people don't object because they love violence or refuse to obey Jesus, but because of a valid concern for protecting their own welfare, and the welfare of their loved ones.

In response to this, some of my fellow pacifists have argued that Christians should simply follow Jesus' way of nonviolence *regardless of the consequences* or whether it makes sense to them. After all, they might protest, "Isn't the way of the cross foolishness? Doesn't Jesus tell us to die to ourselves? We need to follow Jesus regardless of the cost! The way of Jesus goes against our thinking, but we still need to obey even if we don't understand!" they argue.

While this obedience to Jesus is certainly well meant, it is unfortunately reflective of the very same authoritarian religion that Jesus, as we have seen, was so opposed to. Again, the reason Jesus is opposed to this *unquestioning obedience*—even when done in the name of pacifism and a commitment to enemy love—is because it leads to harm.

The simple reality is that we cannot follow something if we don't understand how. This inevitably results in hurtful application because we have no means by which to evaluate what is a correct application, and what is not. That's not the kind of faithfulness Jesus calls us to. Jesus calls us to read the Bible like he does, and that means having a thinking and questioning faith.

Most of us already do this. For example, if I were to ask "Does following Jesus' way of enemy love mean telling women to remain in a situation of domestic abuse?" you would likely respond emphatically, "Heavens no! That's not what Jesus meant!"

This answer reveals that we are not, in fact, blindly following without any regard for whether or not it makes sense to us. We are evaluating. We are seeking to understand. We are wrestling with the text. That's good, because it's the only way to avoid interpretations that hurt people.

As we have seen over and over again, the fruit of *unquestioning obedience* is abuse. This is because *unquestioning obedience* has no way of identifying incorrect and hurtful interpretations, and consequently these are its inevitable result. There's simply no way around this. Until we actually understand the "upside-down kingdom" perspective of Jesus, we will not be able to intelligently apply it to our lives. Obedience is not possible without understanding. Faithfulness cannot exist apart from thought.

Enemy love is indeed counter-cultural, but it is by no means unrealistic or illogical. Nor is it opposed to a healthy desire to care for and protect ourselves and our loved ones. So if you are feeling resistant to the way of enemy love because of a concern to protect your own safety and the safety of those you love, please hear me say that this is a good and valid concern which I share with you. Jesus cares for us and is not calling us to passivity or irresponsibility. Enemy love is about ending suffering, not validating it.

HOW TO MISREAD JESUS

Over the centuries many people—in an attempt to faithfully follow in the way of enemy love—have tragically misinterpreted the words of Jesus, understanding them as demanding us to do things that seem deeply hurtful—telling people to passively submit to oppression, to not defend themselves or those who are being hurt and wronged. When we read some of the words of Jesus at face value, it's easy to see how one could get this impression:

> If your right hand causes you to stumble, cut it off and throw it away. It is better for you to lose one part of your body than for your whole body to go into hell. (Matt 5:30)

> If anyone comes to me and does not hate his father and mother, his wife and children, his brothers and sisters—yes, even his own life—he cannot be my disciple. (Luke 14:26)

Now, we hopefully all know that Jesus was not actually advocating amputation as a method of character development, nor is he suggesting that following him entails self-hatred or being a bad parent. A surefire way to get Jesus horribly wrong is to read him in a wooden and literalistic way that cannot appreciate the subtleties of hyperbole and irony. In the above examples this would result in severed limbs, and an abusive view of ourselves and others.

The primary way Jesus taught was by dramatic *provocation*. He speaks in ironic riddles that tell us to do seemingly absurd things like dying in order to live, and loving the people we hate. Jesus is constantly pulling the rug out from under us—saying things that are intended to shock, to throw us off balance.

Love of enemies seems crazy, and indeed, *it is meant to*. It is deliberately formulated as an ironic paradox—*love those you would normally hate*—in order to provoke us into a radical new way of understanding justice and dealing with conflict. Jesus is *intending* to throw us off balance, to jar us into seeing things from his radically different perspective.

The first step in understanding what Jesus is saying here is to get the irony. If we don't get this we will get Jesus terribly wrong. To read Jesus as *literally* calling us to "hate" our spouse or children is to profoundly misread him. In the same way, when Jesus calls us to "deny ourselves" this equally cannot be read with a wooden literalism, but instead must be understood as a jarring provocation intended to make us re-think our values and assumptions. In questioning these assumptions, Jesus is calling us to be *more* loving, not less.

Once we get this, the next step is to understand what this new perspective of Jesus looks like when it is not expressed in ironic terms. This shift in perspective might broadly be described in terms of moving from a *self-focus* to a *social-focus*. In understanding this, I would propose that the entire concept of *unselfishness* is ultimately an unhelpful one. It is unhelpful because it can give the impression that virtue consists in being *anti*-self (here terms come to mind such as *selfless, self-sacrificing, self-denying,* etc.). This puts the focus in the wrong place—on self.

Instead, a better way to frame the radical perspective of Jesus is a *social-focus*. In other words, our moving away from a self-focused perspective does not entail becoming *anti*-self; rather it entails adopting a relational perspective which *includes* a healthy self-love. A *social-focus* is ultimately self-affirming because we are social beings, and thus can only truly be ourselves *within* relationship. That's why Jesus can make the ironic claim that we "must lose our life to find it" (Matt 10:39) because we must let go of our self-focus in order to truly find our true social selves in relationship.

Again, the change in perspective that Jesus calls us to involves moving from a self-focus to a social-focus. Another way of expressing this shift is moving away from an "us vs. them" perspective to one that excludes no one. That's why Jesus is constantly challenging the "us" of our family, our tribe, our nation, our religion, our group against *them.*

Jesus begins with the call to "love our neighbor *as we love ourselves,*" and then pushes us to expand our definition of "neighbor" to encompass those we would normally reject and shut out. Love of enemies challenges us to enlarge the border of inclusion beyond its normal boundaries of family, tribe, and nation to include those we would regard as unworthy and enemies. In the relational perspective of Jesus, there is no "them," there is only "us."

NEUROSCIENCE AND
THE MIND OF CHRIST

The real difficulty with the practice of enemy love, however, has to do with our emotions. Even if we understand this social-perspective in theory, and desire to interact with others in this way, this social orientation goes completely against the grain of both our thinking and feeling when we are in the midst of conflict.

When we feel threatened, defensive, hurt, or otherwise emotionally triggered our brains automatically override our social-self and jump into self-focus mode. This is often counter-productive because it can block us from finding a solution to our conflict since we can only see things from our self-focused perspective. What's going on, and what can we do about it?

This is something I experience myself: Even though I am deeply committed to Jesus' way of enemy love, when I'm in the middle of an argument with my wife I find myself reverting back into a self-focused and defensive posture. All I can see is *my* perspective, all I can think about is defending *my* rights. I know she's not my enemy, she's my best friend, and yet in the midst of conflict all that seems to go right out the door. What causes us to revert to this self-focused posture? Why is it so hard to think socially when we are feeling hurt or wronged?

In the past decade, neurobiology has made discoveries about the physiology of how our brains work which can help us make sense of what is going on here: When we are feeling threatened, triggered, and emotionally flooded this activates the amygdala, which is the part of the brain involved in the processing of raw emotions such as anger and fear.

The amygdala is essentially the brain's watchtower, and when it is fired up in alarm mode, it sends out neurochemicals which effectively shut down the prefrontal cortex. The prefrontal cortex is the part of your brain associated with things like relational connection, empathy, impulse control, self-reflection, moral judgment and conscience—in short, the part of your brain in charge of what we might call the *social-self*. Bottom line: When we feel threatened or triggered, the compassionate and social part of our brain literally gets shut down.[77]

The brain's "shut-down" mechanism has a practical survival function: It means that when we are in danger our brain kicks into alarm mode which can save our life in situations of immediate peril. However, it also means that when we get triggered in an argument with a loved one, the smart and compassionate part of our brain is temporarily turned off, which can make us do and say hurtful things.

When we are unaware of this, we can get swept up in those feelings. Rather than responding thoughtfully and with compassion, we can become emotionally reactive—triggered. Our brain will even attempt to rationalize these feelings and tell us that it is *right* and *just* to respond this way.

---

77 For a fascinating and readable study of this, see Daniel J. Siegel, *Mindsight: The New Science of Personal Transformation* (New York: Bantam Books, 2011).

Love of enemies is about breaking out of the thinking of our fear-based primitive brain, and instead learning to engage our higher social brain again—thinking relationally. When we learn how to do that, we can break the hostile dynamic that it is so easy to get sucked into.

To illustrate this, let me share an example from everyday life: The other day our 5-year-old daughter had a "meltdown." She's screaming, and I'm feeling triggered. My amygdala has kicked in now, but I do my best to pull myself together, and, taking her by the hand, I bring her to her room for a time-out. When we get there, she screams at me hysterically, demanding I give her a hug.

Now mind you, I'm not feeling compassion right then—I'm mad. In my head I'm rationalizing that emotion, thinking, "I don't want to reward this selfish behavior with a hug!" So I feel tempted to pull away from her, thinking it would be good for her to feel bad so she could "learn her lesson." In my self-focused amygdala state, my instinct was to withhold love from her. I then rationalized and justified this in my mind, arguing that this was responsible parenting. I told myself it was "for her own good."

But something in me knew—as much as I didn't feel like doing it at the time—that she really did need that hug. So even though I didn't feel like it, I put my arms around her and held her. And when I did, a miniature miracle happened: All her distress, panic, and rage just melted away. She was able to calm down, and able to listen as we talked about what had happened.

183

Later, when I was able to reflect on this, I could see that my reluctant act of kindness was not reinforcing bad behavior, but just the opposite: It had allowed her to come to her senses again. Making her feel bad would have only pushed her deeper into her self-focused panic, triggering her amygdala. She needed that hug —and the sense of security it gave her—to be able to break out of the emotional fit she was in. Neurologically speaking, the embrace had a regulating effect, calming her nervous system. It allowed her to be relational again.

This simple act of kindness broke the hurtful dynamic my daughter and I were both caught in. That's the core working principle of enemy love: Do not be overcome by anger, but overcome anger with kindness; do not get sucked into mirroring hurt, but instead break the cycle by responding in the opposite spirit. As the prayer of St. Francis says,

> where there is hatred, let me sow love
> where there is injury, pardon
> where there is doubt, faith
> where there is despair, hope
> where there is darkness, light
> and where there is sadness, joy.

Instead of responding *in kind*, we respond with a restorative action that reverses the hurtful dynamic. This results in bringing us out of our self-focused antagonistic us/them mentality, and instead putting us in a relational mindset where we can think socially, and compassionately.

While hugging my daughter helped her regain her relational focus, no one had given me a hug, and so I had to go against my reactive impulses and choose to absorb her anger, rather than getting dragged into it. That's hard to do when we are feeling emotionally triggered. Our brains aren't wired that way. In the heat of conflict our minds become clouded with pride and pain. Because we feel threatened, our primary goal becomes self-preservation at the expense of a relational orientation. Our brain goes into emergency self-protection mode, and shuts down our ability to think wisely and socially.

Along the same lines, it would be equally natural for a paramedic witnessing the mayhem of blood and injured bodies at the scene of an accident to become overwhelmed and freeze. First responders however must learn to overcome these natural impulses so they can work to save lives. In order to rise above our natural response of emotional reactivity in the midst of conflict we need to develop similar skills—working to respond thoughtfully and socially, rather than react emotionally.

Paul tells us that as we walk in this way of the Spirit, we will be "transformed by the renewing of our minds." Neuroscience confirms that Paul was on to something big: It's a concept known as *neuroplasticity*, which refers the brain's ability to change itself based on our experiences. Amazingly, our brain actually structurally changes, based on the input it receives, creating new synaptic linkages and even growing new neurons.

This means that, as we learn to engage our thinking and social prefrontal cortex in times of stress, our brain re-wires itself over time to be more naturally compassionate and social, and less driven by our "carnal" reactive emotions. We are quite literally transformed by the renewing of our minds through neuroplasticity.

The first step to this is having the humility to recognize that when we are feeling defensive and emotionally triggered we may simply need time to allow our prefrontal cortex to come back on line. Just as we need to have the maturity to recognize when we've had too much to drink and hand over our car keys, similarly, when we're "under the influence" of the amygdala, we need to recognize that the smart and social part of our brain is *impaired.* That's why—even when we believe in and are committed to the way of enemy love—we can so easily find ourselves reverting back into a self-focused and defensive posture when we are feeling threatened, hurt, or triggered.

This discrepancy can lead to feelings of guilt and failure. Am I a bad Christian? We can feel like Paul must have when he writes, "I do not understand what I do. For what I want to do I do not do, but what I hate I do. As it is, it is no longer I myself who do it, but it is sin living in me. For I know that good itself does not dwell in me, that is, in my sinful nature ... For in my inner being I delight in God's law; but I see another law at work in me, waging war against the law of my mind and making me a prisoner of the law of sin at work within me" (Rom 7:14-23).

Today, because of the insights of neuroscience, we know something that Paul did not in his pre-scientific perspective: The problem is not moral; it is physiological. The moral part is *what we do with those feelings*.

Sometimes we can manage to break through our amygdala reaction right then, acting socially to disarm the conflict, as I was able to do in the above example with my daughter. But it can be an equally appropriate response to simply remove ourselves from the situation—giving ourselves time and space to calm down, and allowing our prefrontal cortex to come back on line.

With parenting this might mean asking our spouse to step in, or perhaps giving ourselves a parental "time-out" by listening to some music with headphones on our iPod. Sometimes the wisest response when we are feeling emotionally flooded is simply having the maturity and humility to recognize our limits and giving ourselves a break. After all, as Paul says, forbearance and self-control are part of the fruits of the spirit too.

RE-THINKING CRIME AND PUNISHMENT

Crime stirs up lots of emotions for us. For some this is expressed in a desire for retribution. We want to make those hurt who hurt us. Again, it is perfectly reasonable that we want to feel safe. The question is whether our current criminal justice system with its focus on retribution and punishment is the best way to accomplish this.

We commonly think of justice in terms of retribution. When we speak of a person "getting justice" we mean getting punishment. Love of enemies challenges this understanding of justice and asks: What if justice was not about punishing and hurting, but about mending and making things right again? What if justice was not about deterring through negative consequences, but about doing something good in order to reverse those hurtful dynamics? What if real justice was about repairing broken lives?

This is an opposing understanding of justice known as *restorative justice*. Restorative justice is a justice that works to repair. Unlike retributive justice which is almost exclusively focused on the offender, restorative justice is primarily focused on addressing the needs of victims, focusing on what their needs are and how offenders can take responsibility to repair and make things right.[78]

Working towards the reform and rehabilitation of criminals is not merely a matter of compassion; it is a matter of societal self-interest. The sad fact is that our current prison system has become a factory for hardening criminals rather than healing them. Instead of learning empathy and how to manage their impulses and emotions, the brutal culture of prison life teaches inmates that one must be brutally violent in order to survive. Because of these patterns learned in prison, the alarming repeat

---

78 Howard Zehr, *Changing Lenses: A New Focus for Crime and Justice* (Scottdale, PA: Herald, 2005).

offense rate is sadly not at all surprising.[79] Locking someone up in the hell of prison life naturally breeds violence, not reform or repentance. People do not learn empathy by being shamed and dehumanized. Retribution gains popular support by appealing to our most primitive impulses, but in the end results in a broken system that perpetuates hurt and cycles of violence.

So what is the alternative? In contrast to this dire picture of our dysfunctional penal system, consider the alternative approach of the San Francisco Sheriff's Department's RSVP program which is based on a restorative justice model. The RSVP program works with societies most violent men—wife beaters, murderers, and gang bangers—helping them to look into the mirror, and face themselves and their violence.

Rather than simply spending their time behind bars, stewing in resentment in their cell or interacting with the toxic prison culture of violence in the yard, these men learn in a community to become self-reflective, developing empathy, and finding healthy ways of managing their emotions. These violent men learn for the first time how to maintain their own dignity and respect without demeaning or harming others.

The results are striking: The RSVP program boasts a staggering 80% reduction of violent recidivism. Additionally, it has seen a dramatic reduction of inmate violence as well. For

---

79 According to a 2011 Pew study, more than four in ten offenders nationwide return to state prison within three years of their release. Despite a massive increase in state spending on prisons in excess of $50 billion a year, recidivism rates have remained virtually unchanged between 1994 and 2007. Pew Center on the States, *State of Recidivism: The Revolving Door of America's Prisons* (Washington, DC: The Pew Charitable Trusts, April 2011).

example, while it was typical to have ca. 60 assaults on officers per year before, in the RSVP dorm these were completely eliminated.[80] In other words, it not only makes society safer, it makes the guards safer as well.

The RSVP program serves as a powerful illustration of how love of enemies can be effectively applied on a governmental and institutional level. What is critical to understand here is that this is not a matter of ignoring justice. On the contrary, it is precisely a matter of bringing about true justice by working to repair, rather than perpetuating harm. This is restorative justice.

THE DYNAMICS OF NONVIOLENCE

This brings us to a distinction that is often drawn between governments and individuals. The basic argument is that while individuals should turn the other cheek, this cannot be expected of governments because they have an obligation to protect their citizens.

The error here is assuming that love of enemies involves passively allowing oneself or others to be wronged. The reality however is that it is just as irresponsible and wrong to ask an

---

80 Sunny Swartz, *Dreams from the Monster Factory* (New York: Scribner, 2009). RSVP was also featured on the PBS show *Visionaries* (episode 1106) *http://www.youtube.com/watch?v=HDAelT3K5w4*

individual to ignore harm as it would be to do this on an institutional level. That's not what nonviolence is about.

Both on an individual and an institutional level the way of Jesus must be applied in a way that results in reducing violence rather than legitimizing it. The goal of enemy love is not to subject oneself to violence, but to act to break the cycle of violence. Love of enemies is therefore equally applicable both on an interpersonal level, and on larger governmental and societal levels.

That said, I would propose that, in applying this, it is critical to make a distinction between *love of enemies* and *turning the other cheek*. The two are not synonymous, and it is important to recognize the difference.

Love of enemies is a general principle, applicable to both individuals and society, which has many different context-specific applications. Turning the other cheek is one particular application of the larger principle of enemy love. As such, it can be deeply effective in its proper context, but irresponsible and wrong in others. To understand this distinction, we will need to take a closer look at the proper context of turning the other cheek.

When people speak of nonviolence, nine times out of ten, what they are thinking of is *nonviolent resistance. This is turning the other cheek applied on a corporate scale.* Two names that immediately come to mind here are Gandhi and Martin Luther King. What is less well-known is that beginning in the 1980s—for the first time in human history—nonviolent resistance campaigns successfully toppled multiple oppressive regimes across the globe, often in the face of overwhelming military power and brutality.

A recent study compared the outcomes of 323 nonviolent and violent resistance campaigns from 1900 to 2006, and found that major nonviolent campaigns were effective 53% of the time, whereas violent ones only worked 26% of the time.[81] In other words, while nonviolent resistance does not always work, it is twice as effective as violent resistance.

These statistical findings certainly go against what is often claimed in public discourse and the media. So often we see the storyline rehearsed in Hollywood movies that the only way to deal with "bad guys" is with violence. Apparently the idea that dictators "only respond to (violent) force" simply is not true. The facts demonstrate that nonviolent resistance appears to be a more powerful force.

Why is nonviolent resistance so effective where violence fails? The study suggests that one notable factor is something Gene Sharp has called *political jujitsu*, where "an unjust act—often violent repression—recoils against its originators, often resulting in the breakdown of obedience among regime supporters, mobilization of the population against the regime, and international condemnation of the regime."[82]

---

81 Maria J. Stephan and Erica Chenoweth, "Why Civil Resistance Works" *International Security*, 33:1 (Summer 2008), 7–44.

82 "Why Civil Resistance Works" 11.

Sharp's groundbreaking work in systemizing the methods of nonviolent resistance has served as a blueprint which has been adopted by activists throughout the world, and the results have been staggering: Dictators have fallen and people living in oppression have overcome, without bloodshed.[83]

In the context of a people seeking to overcome oppression, nonviolent resistance—the way of turning the other cheek—has shown itself not only to be a viable alternative to violence, but a much more effective one. However, in the wrong context, it would not only be ineffective but wrong. For example, imagine asking a prison guard to apply this same principle of turning the other cheek as a way of dealing with prison violence—placing themselves defenseless between fighting inmates. One could rightfully argue that this would be not only unreasonable, but morally irresponsible.

So what's the difference? Why wouldn't nonviolent resistance work in the context of prison violence? The reason is simple: *Because the power dynamic is completely reversed.* In nonviolent resistance the power dynamic is one of an oppressed people struggling for social justice against those in power. In a prison setting the guards are the ones holding the power.

Turning the other cheek (i.e. nonviolent resistance) is a context-specific application which is not always appropriate in every situation. Because of the power dynamic involved, it would therefore be inappropriate for a nation to practice turning the

---

83 More information on the work of Gene Sharp, as well as free access to his writing, can be found at his website, www.aeinstein.org

other cheek—just as it would be for a prison guard. This does not mean, however, that the broader principle of enemy love cannot be applied here.

To continue with our prison example, as we have seen, programs like RSVP are currently being applied in correctional institutions across the country with great success. In them, guards are not placed in danger. On the contrary, as we saw the RSVP program completely eliminated assaults on officers, creating a safer environment inside the prison system as well as outside.

Like nonviolent resistance, the RSVP program's focus on moral/emotional development (using psycho-education and corrective experiences to build empathy, reflection, self-esteem and impulse control) is a context specific application of enemy love.

While the two approaches differ in their specific methods, they both are examples of enemy love and thus have many similarities. Both act to reverse the cycle of harm, both do this by unmasking and exposing violence, and both ultimately result in societal repair, rather than perpetuating harm. Both are examples of enemy love in action, and both are examples of restorative justice (justice that seeks to make things right, as opposed to justice that seeks to inflict harm). In both the goal is to break the pattern of violence/harm by identifying actions that would break the cycle rather than feeding it.

They differ in the methods by which this is achieved, based on the particular context and social dynamic. The goal therefore would be to identify the power dynamic involved in order to determine the appropriate strategy.

As a final example, consider a situation where the power dynamic is not of a weaker and stronger party at all, but one of two equals—such as a husband and wife having a marital conflict. Nonviolent resistance would obviously be inappropriate here, as would requiring only one partner to receive moral education.

What would be effective, however, is applying methods of nonviolent communication and conflict resolution where each party learns to recognize the legitimate needs of the other, rather than demonizing each other. This has proven to be effective, not only in helping couples work through difficulties, but also in resolving conflict between rival people groups and nations caught in spirals of retaliation.[84]

Again, in each context, the key is identifying the pattern of violence/harm involved, and then acting to reverse that cycle— repairing rather than retaliating. This applies not only to massive issues like taking down dictatorships and reforming violent criminals, but equally to how we go about our daily lives.

The task therefore is to pay attention to the dynamics in everyday situations—in how we interact with our partners, how we raise our kids, how we conduct business—working out how to actively promote peace and justice in each particular context.

---

84 For a fuller treatment of effective strategies in dealing with international conflict, see Glen Stassen *Just Peacemaking: Transforming Initiatives for Justice and Peace* (Louisville: Westminster/John Knox, 1998).

CONCLUSION

In this chapter, we've looked at a number of obstacles that hinder us from the practice of enemy love. The first obstacle we explored were the many misconceptions we have of what love of enemies means—some even coming from (a misunderstanding of) the words of Jesus himself.

These misconceptions all revolve around the mistaken idea that love of enemies entails not caring for ourselves or those we love. Believing that love of enemies is negligent and hurtful, many people do not practice it. The alternative is not to demand their unquestioned obedience, because this will result in a hurtful application. Instead it is critical that we seek to have a practical understanding of how to apply enemy love properly.

A major issue that plays into this is that the issues here are not primarily intellectual but emotional. These are questions that affect one of the most powerful drives we humans posses—our survival instinct, the will to live. To threaten this strikes at the most basic needs in Maslow's Hierarchy: the preservation of life, our need for safety, the need for love and belonging, our need for self-esteem and dignity.

When a person fears that these core needs are threatened, that's when the amygdala kicks in, overriding our cerebral cortex (our social brain). This fact of how our brains function is what makes thinking socially on the one hand so obvious when we can step back and reflect, and yet so impossible in the heat of conflict since our thinking- and social-brain is literally shut down.

It can seem like "dying to yourself" when we are in that self-focused amygdala state, like "foolishness" and "weakness," but really it's just about learning to think socially. This primal emotional reaction is also why discussions about nonviolence so often result in people becoming hyper-emotional and their thinking-brains shutting down.

A major part of the task therefore is to get past the reactionary responses of our primitive-brain (the limbic system), and to learn to engage our reflective social-brain (the cerebral cortex) in order to find solutions to our problems. Our policies of how we deal with crime or when we go to war should not be driven by fear-based reactive emotional responses, yet the media and our politicians often present these issues in precisely this manner, playing off of people's emotional reactivity and fear.

It must be stressed that the desire to protect our own life and the lives of those we love is something profoundly good and important. It's essential to our survival and well-being. Our limbic system thus serves a vital life-preserving function. The question we need to ask ourselves is: What is the best way to fulfill these needs in our complex social world?

As we have seen, our brain's drive for self-preservation can become counter-productive, actually blocking us from the relational connection and love we need as social beings. Adopting the relational perspective of enemy love does not at all mean

197

denying these needs. On the contrary, it's about meeting them in better ways—ways that work for all of us.

The basic working principle here is that conflict typically spirals into patterns of hurting and being hurt. The goal is to determine what is needed to break that cycle of harm, rather than fueling it—asking what we can do to repair (restorative justice), rather than adding to the injury and perpetuating the cycle of harm/violence (retributive justice).

This applies not only to our interpersonal relationships, but just as much to how we deal with societal issues, several of which we have explored in this chapter. These examples of course do not cover all the possible scenarios where love of enemies could be applied in our world. That would easily require a book of its own (if not several books!). However, these real life examples do serve to debunk the popular myth that love of enemies cannot be effectively applied on a state or societal level. The many examples demonstrate that they *are* working.

Faithfully following Jesus along the trajectory he has set involves working towards a society that moves away from retribution which perpetuates harm and towards restorative justice which acts to make things right, valuing everyone, helping us all to act compassionately and responsibly.

The fact is, we no longer have to imagine how Jesus' way of enemy love *could* work, we simply need to inform ourselves about the many ways that restorative justice and nonviolence *are* working in our world, and learn to join in.

CHAPTER 9

UNDOING JUDGMENT

In contrast to the way of justifying human acts of violence as a means of bringing about a just world, Jesus and the New Testament present a radically different way to bring about justice by making things right, reversing patterns of harm and violence through acts of compassion and care. We see in the New Testament the first steps in this direction, and our faithfulness requires that we continue in that same direction in our time. This applies to the issue of slavery as well as to the issue of state violence (punishing crime and engaging in war).

In broad terms we might say that while the Old Testament commands humans to commit violence in God's name— including attempted genocide—the New Testament categorically forbids this for the people of God.

It can hardly be expressed how huge this step is. The New Testament must be regarded as a first step along a trajectory in regards to changing oppressive societal structures which at the time as a persecuted minority group they had little power to change. Finding ourselves in a position to effect those changes in society today, our task is to work out how to apply the spirit of Jesus' teaching to our time and circumstance.

If there is an issue of violence in the New Testament at all, it is not one of humans committing violence in God's name, but rather the issue of God's violence expressed in the form of divine judgment. This leads us to ask some difficult questions:

Is God violent, while we are commanded not to be?

Are we called to forgive, while God judges and condemns people to hell?

In a general sense it makes sense to argue that God is on a level above us, and so alone has the right to do what we cannot— to judge and to punish. However, in the context of the New Testament this argument falls apart because both Paul and Jesus explicitly present God as our model for enemy love. Jesus tells us that we are to love our enemies so "that you may be children of your Father in heaven. He causes his sun to rise on the evil and the good, and sends rain on the righteous and the unrighteous ... Be perfect, therefore, as your heavenly Father is perfect" (Matt 5:43–48).

Jesus is reversing a passage here from Deuteronomy which declares that God sends rain to the righteous and withholds it from sinners:

> If you faithfully obey the commands I am giving you today ... then I will send rain on your land ... Be careful, or you will be enticed to turn away ... Then the LORD's anger will burn against you, and he will shut up the heavens so that it will not rain. (Deut 11:13–17)

Jesus, in contrast, is saying that God does not repay evil for evil and good for good, but instead that God shows unconditional benevolence. This isn't just about weather, it constitutes a complete overturning of the Old Testament's understanding of quid pro quo justice. Jesus dismisses that this kind of justice is something "even pagans do" and thus not a true expression of God's righteousness. If we want to love like God, Jesus says, then we need to love our enemies. God is our model for this kind of love.

Just as Jesus sees the source of enemy love in God, Paul too presents God as the ultimate example of enemy love in action, "God demonstrates his own love for us in this: While we were still sinners, Christ died for us ... while we were God's enemies, we were reconciled to him through the death of his Son" (Rom 5:8, 10).

So while advocates of violence and retribution may think that God has a different standard of morality than Jesus does, this is simply not what the New Testament claims. *Jesus and Paul both see God as our model of enemy love.* That means that God does not have a different standard of morality than we do. Rather, God in Christ reveals the way of enemy love that we are to follow. God is Christlike. If you have seen Jesus, you have seen the Father.

Michael Gorman makes the powerful argument that while God alone has the right to judge, God instead in Christ *gives up that right* and chooses the way of enemy love, acting to save and redeem humanity through an act of nonviolent self-sacrifice. God has a right to status, but forgoes that right, taking on human flesh and dying on a cross to save us.

This "master narrative" of God's way in Christ in turn becomes the model for our way.[85] The way of nonviolence, radical forgiveness, and enemy love we are called to is one that is modeled after God's character revealed in Christ.

---

85 Michael J. Gorman, *Inhabiting the Cruciform God* (Grand Rapids: Eerdmans, 2009), 155–158.

Parables as Paradox

Now if that's all true, if Jesus in fact reveals the heart of the Father to us, then why do the descriptions of God's judgment in the New Testament often sound so... well... un-Christlike?

Let's begin with one of the most challenging passages in the New Testament, the parable of the unmerciful servant in Matthew 18:21–35. Jesus tells the story here of a king who forgives his servant for a huge debt, but then when the king hears that this servant has refused to forgive a very small debt, the king becomes enraged. Jesus describes how the king then hands the servant over "to the jailers to be tortured, until he should pay back all he owed." and then concludes with the haunting pronouncement, "This is how my heavenly Father will treat each of you unless you forgive your brother or sister from your heart" (v. 35).

Now, in this parable, the debt of 10,000 talents that the servant owed was completely unpayable, amounting to about 200,000 years' wages.[86] This amount is so exaggerated, it's almost humorous. Similarly, a talent was the highest unit of currency, and 10,000 (Greek: *myrios*) was the largest numeral in the Greek language. So together "10,000 talents" was the largest sum of money one could think of, comparable perhaps to our saying "he owed him a zillion dollars" today. In other words, it was an

---

86 In the parable the servant is owed 100 denarii. A denarius is a day's wages, so he is owed about half a year's wages. In comparison his debt of 10,000 talents would be 60 million denarii or about 200,000 years' wages.

absurdly large debt that would have been impossible to pay off—least of all from prison. So if the servant was to be "tortured" in prison "until he paid back all he owed," he would not be getting out any time soon.

If we jump back a few verses we can see that the reason Jesus tells this parable is in response to a question from Peter who asks Jesus, "How many times must I forgive, seven times?" Jesus answers him, "No, seventy-seven times" (v. 21-22), and then proceeds to tell the above parable to illustrate this point.

Jesus here is lampooning a declaration of escalating vengeance from the Old Testament, "If Cain is avenged seven times, then Lamech seventy-seven times!" (Gen 4:24). Jesus takes this one-upmanship of escalating violence and playfully turns this familiar phrase into an escalation of forgiveness, similar to how our popular phrase "random acts of kindness" humorously reverses the idea of "random acts of violence."

Now, this is a story told in broad and exaggerated strokes. It is not meant to be a realistic depiction of financial debt. Rather, it is an intentionally exaggerated scenario, intended to drive home Jesus' point to Peter about unlimited forgiveness. It dramatically —and perhaps even humorously—illustrates how wrong it would be for us not to forgive another for some trivial slight when we have been forgiven such an unbelievably huge debt by God.

The trouble comes when we take this simple story, with its broadly painted strokes, and begin to pore over every minute detail like a lawyer reading the fine print. This may seem like the right way to read Scripture, and it is certainly seen in many Bible commentaries which go on for page after page discussing a single word. Indeed, this can be a valuable practice at times, but the danger here is that we end up stretching this simple illustration beyond its intended limits, and as a result end up with a conclusion that is the very *opposite* of what Jesus was trying to convey to Peter.

Do we seriously think that the point Jesus was trying to get across is that we should forgive 77 times—that is, without measure—while God in contrast will forgive us just once, and then after that the gloves come off and it's "payback time"? Read in this way, we would have to conclude that God does not even forgive seven times like Peter had suggested. *Just one chance and then that's it.* Is that really the point Jesus was trying to make? Do we seriously think that Jesus was intending to teach that we are more merciful than God?

Looking at the broader context it is clear that the moral of this parable (and Matthew's intent in ordering it here in this pericope) is clearly not intended to imply that God is less merciful than we are. Jesus has just answered Peter's question of the limits of forgiveness by challenging him to practice the escalation of love. This parable is meant to drive that point home by illustrating how bad it would be for us not to forgive others when we have been forgiven such a great debt by God. We should treat others with the same grace that we need, and which God has richly shown us.

205

This is clearly the main point of this parable, and, based on the cultural understandings of the people at the time, this point would have been clear to Jesus' original audience. They would not have had the problems we have with the unmerciful actions of the king because they would expect kings to treat servants this way. However, we stumble over this picture.

It is worth considering why it is that we stumble here. It may not be the intended point in the original context, but for us today it becomes a major stumbling block—especially since the figure of the angry king is directly compared to God. It may not be the main point, but it is still there. What are we to make of this? Is the problem that we are projecting our "modern sensitivities" onto the text?

In this parable Jesus compares God to a king who—in the way kings did at the time—flies into a rage and orders torture for an ungrateful servant. Yet if we keep reading in Matthew, we see that a couple chapters later, Jesus questions the entire idea of comparing God to a king at all:

> You know that the rulers of the Gentiles lord it over them, and their high officials exercise authority over them. Not so with you. Instead, whoever wants to become great among you must be your servant, and whoever wants to be first must be your slave— just as the Son of Man did not come to be served, but to serve, and to give his life as a ransom for many. (Matt 20:25-28)

Jesus models the way of God for us, not as one who "lords it over others," but as the *servant Lord*, and calls for us to embody that way too. Following Jesus means rejecting the way of domination—it means rejecting the way of kings. If Jesus reveals God, then he reveals that *God is not like a king at all.*

To the extent that you have embraced that idea, you will stumble over the above parable of the king and his ungrateful servant. You will read "God is like an angry king" and think "No, Jesus teaches us that God is not at all like a king, God is like a suffering servant," and you would be absolutely right!

In each of his parables, Jesus is turning our thinking upside down. That's the nature of how his parables function: They are simple stories with familiar settings and characters that involve an ironic twist. That twist is intended to provoke us to see things differently.

Jesus does the same sort of thing with his provocative statements of reversal: *lose your life to find it, love your enemies, and here: the greatest is the servant of all.* These are likewise intended to take a familiar concept and turn it on its ear, making us rethink our assumptions.

So in Matthew 18 Jesus begins by turning the idea of payback on its head, playfully reversing Lamech's escalation of violence with his own escalation of mercy. He follows this with a parable to illustrate the idea that we should be generous with forgiveness because God has generously forgiven us.

This parable is set in the familiar social settings of a king and his slave—a scenario that was all too familiar to his original audience at the time. But then, a couple chapters later, Jesus similarly dismantles that understanding of greatness, reversing the balance of power between master and servant, and in doing so redefining how we see God: God is the servant. Power is about lifting people up, not pushing them down.

Now take a look at what Jesus is doing here: Not only is he dismantling our traditional concepts of what justice and power are about—*he is at the same time progressively dismantling the traditional story-world of his own parables* couched in the cultural assumptions of his time.

Once we have embraced Jesus' understanding of servant lordship, we cannot accept the crude comparison of God to a volatile dictator because Jesus has dismantled that worldly understanding of power. Once we have read Matthew 20, we cannot read Matthew 18 the same way again. Our problem is not that we are projecting our "modern sensitivities," but rather that our hearts have been progressively shaped by the values of Jesus.

Each parable begins within the confines of the worldly assumptions of the people. It begins there within their familiar world of kings and slaves and torture, and then introduces a radical new idea into the mix, a twist in the familiar scenario which flips one of those ideas on its head—one idea at a time, toppling them like dominos.

Therefore, the more we embrace these ideas of Jesus' "upside-down kingdom," the more we will have trouble with the worldly assumptions that these very parables are situated in. That's not because we are disagreeing with Jesus here, but precisely *because* our values have been shaped by his parables and teaching. That's *why* we question the validity of a king that doesn't act like Christ. *We reject it because Jesus taught us to.*

We can therefore embrace the idea of forgiving a great debt (which is the point Jesus is making in the parable of the ungrateful servant), while rejecting the idea that God is a torturing dictator, which reflects the worldview assumptions of his first century audience—assumptions Jesus rejects, not only two chapters later in Matthew 20, but also in his broader understanding of God as the one who is our model for enemy love.

UNTEACHING HELL

The above is an example of reading Jesus on a trajectory. This entails recognizing the direction Jesus is moving us in, and differentiating this from the starting point in the familiar cultural assumptions that his parables are couched in.

Jesus is progressively dismantling the cultural assumptions that his own parables are set in, replacing them one by one with kingdom ideas instead. Again, this is how his parables function:

They begin in the familiar setting of those cultural assumptions, and then push us to re-think some aspect of that, introducing us instead to a kingdom principle.

Similarly, when we read statements about "hell" and "torture" in those parables, we need to ask whether these are the main point Jesus is trying to convey or whether they are perhaps instead part of the scenery, reflective of the familiar cultural and religious assumptions of his audience—just as the assumed legitimacy of slavery and dictatorship are—which Jesus is working to dismantle bit by bit, one parable at a time.

For example, consider the parable of the sheep and goats just a few chapters later in Matthew 25:31-46. This is a classic prooftext for those who wish to promote the idea of God's punishment and judgment in hell. Here Jesus tells a story of the final judgment in which he makes some seemingly harsh declarations, "Depart from me, you who are cursed, into the eternal fire prepared for the devil and his angels" (v. 41).

Again, we need to begin by asking here what the central point is that Jesus is seeking to illustrate. As all parables do, this one begins in familiar territory, in this case in the assumed familiar setting of Jewish apocalyptic, which was reflective of his audience's conception of the day of reckoning.

Yet, once again, Jesus is turning the tables on their expectations. Jesus tells his religious audience that they won't get in because they are part of the right race or religion as they expected, but rather they will be judged by how they loved the least, by how they showed compassion, by how they loved their enemies.

Jesus here completely redefines what makes a person "in" or "out." You are "in" if you care for those who are "out." In doing this, Jesus is not affirming this segregation, but provocatively tearing down the very barrier separating insiders from outsiders. He is undoing the very idea of exclusion. As Jesus does over and over with his parables, here again we see Jesus beginning with a common assumption (the image of the final judgment) and then turning that familiar idea on its head: In the upside-down kingdom of the servant-lord you show your allegiance to God by how you love those who are condemned. *Jesus is not confirming judgment, he is undoing it.*

We can see this pattern repeating over and over: Jesus is not in fact teaching "this is the way hell is" any more than he is teaching "God is like an emotionally imbalanced dictator." Rather, these were the *people's* assumptions at the time in that culture. This was *their* starting point. Jesus begins with their perspective, and pulls the rug out from under them by creatively inserting a radical new idea focused on grace that serves to upend and subvert the entire system.

The more we attune ourselves to the kingdom thinking of Jesus—which is constantly causing us to re-think our prejudices and assumptions—the more we will have trouble with the violent world of retribution that these parables are set in.

Again, recall how a trajectory reading functions: from the perspective of the people at the time he is moving them forward away from notions of exclusion and unforgiveness. However looking back from our Jesus-formed values the starting point of these parables can appear regressive. We therefore need to identify where Jesus was moving and ask how this might apply to us.

We need to adopt a trajectory reading that both remains sensitive to the potential violence in the assumed worldview of the parables, and at the same time recognizes the redemptive possibility of such passages when read within the larger narrative context of the way of Jesus' message of enemy love.

Put differently, we need, on the one hand, to understand the point of the parables as they would have been heard in their original context without, on the other hand, becoming insensitive to the very real ethical problems that their culturally-bound violent imagery can evoke for us today—especially when we have adopted the values of Jesus which are diametrically opposed to these cultural assumptions.

This entails adopting both a *hermeneutic of trust* and a *hermeneutic of suspicion*. The hermeneutic of trust allows us to identify the original intent of promoting compassion within its cultural context, while the hermeneutic of suspicion allows us to push forward towards its intended trajectory *beyond* that cultural context of violent retribution, embracing a fuller image of God's true nature revealed in Christ as our ultimate model of enemy love.

Jesus puts us on this redemptive trajectory by revealing God's heart characterized by unconditional enemy love. It is vital that we recognize this direction of grace and enemy love that Jesus is pointing us towards. To miss this is to miss the very point of the parables. Navigating this involves the difficult task of sorting out the cultural baggage—where Jesus begins—from the trajectory of grace that Jesus is pushing us towards. This involves the interpretive art of recognizing the difference between the flower of the gospel, and the socio-religious soil it grew out of.

MATTHEW'S USE OF VIOLENT LANGUAGE

The above perspective makes sense of the social setting of Jesus' parables, identifying how Jesus is moving away from their worldly assumptions, setting a trajectory towards grace and enemy love. However, it is also striking that many of the parables seem to be clothed in violent descriptions of God's judgment, emphasizing divine retribution and the suffering of the damned with an apparent relish. What are we to make of this?

It's important to note here that this is not characteristic of all of the Gospels, but of one in particular: the Gospel of Matthew. With the exception of Luke 13:28, all of the "weeping and gnashing of teeth" passages are unique to Matthew (Matt 8:12; 13:42, 50; 22:13; 24:51; 25:30).

For example, in Luke's telling of the story of the faith of the centurion we read "When Jesus heard this, he was amazed at him, and turning to the crowd following him, he said, "I tell you, I have not found such great faith even in Israel" (Luke 7:9). Matthew's version reads the same, "When Jesus heard this, he was amazed and said to those following him, 'Truly I tell you, I have not found anyone in Israel with such great faith," but then appends this ending:

> "I say to you that many will come from the east and the west, and will take their places at the feast with Abraham, Isaac and Jacob in the kingdom of heaven. *But the subjects of the kingdom will be thrown outside, into the darkness, where there will be weeping and gnashing of teeth."* (Matt 8:10–12)

Matthew inserts the above phrase, marked in italics, frequently, alternating between the ending "thrown into darkness" and "thrown into the blazing furnace." In parallel passages telling the same stories in the other Gospels these phrases are absent, indicating that they have been added by Matthew.

Similarly, references to "the fire of hell" (Matt 5:22), "the eternal fire prepared for the devil" (Matt 25:41), and "eternal punishment" (Matt 25:46) appear only in Matthew's Gospel.[87] In

---

87 The only exceptions to this are the story of Lazarus and the rich man (Luke 16:19-31), a reference to "Gehenna" in the hyperbolic statement of Jesus involving severing

other words, while the concept of being in a state of lostness and condemnation are found in the other Gospels, the idea of eternal punishment with an emphasis on vengeance and violent suffering seems to be unique to Matthew.

Alongside this is the frequent use of violent imagery which, again, stands out as unique in Matthew. We read of the unfaithful being "tortured" (Matt 18:34), "tied hand and foot" (Matt 22:13), "cut to pieces" (Matt 24:51, par. Luke 12:46), "thrown into darkness" (Matt 8:12; 22:13; 25:30), and "thrown into the blazing furnace" (Matt 13:42 & 50).

Considering the prevalence of this violent language in Matthew, together with its virtual absence in the parallel accounts of the other synoptic Gospels, it is hard to avoid the conclusion that these are not original to Jesus, but are instead Matthew's own embellishments.

Now, simply because Matthew has augmented the story of Jesus is, in itself, not a reason to reject it. Indeed, while it is hard to deny that Matthew has embellished the words of Jesus— adding violent language that is absent in the other parallel Gospel accounts—one could equally make the argument that he likewise has added to the words of Jesus on the Sermon on the Mount. That is, we find in Matthew's *amplification* of Jesus both some of the most troubling parts of the New Testament, as well as some of the most inspired and beautiful passages.

---

limbs rather than sinning (Mark 9:43-48, par. Matt 18:8-9), and a general warning to fear God "who can destroy body and soul in hell" (Luke 12:5). While the other Gospels contain these references, Matthew's depictions stand out for their emphasis on suffering and retribution, while the others simply serve as warnings.

If our criterion is one based purely on historical "authenticity" then we would be in danger of throwing the baby out with the bathwater: We would lose the "hellfire" passages, and lose the Sermon on the Mount with it. But is historical "authenticity" really the question we should be asking here? Let's be honest: The problem is not so much *who* said it, but *what* is being said. That is, the question we really need to be asking is: *Is this good?*

The real question we need to be asking is the question of a disciple, not of an academic historian. What we ultimately need to ask is: Has Matthew accurately captured the spirit of Jesus with his particular "amplifications" in the form of the threat of God's end-time judgment or in the seeming relish with which he describes the future demise of the unrighteous? Is it possible that Matthew's violent additions to the Jesus-story are a reflection of the worldly religious thought-world that Jesus was trying to move us *away* from, and that Matthew was perhaps, to some degree, still captive to?

These are difficult questions, but the first step to finding answers is having the moral courage to ask them. What I hope to show in the remainder of this chapter is that learning to read Matthew on a trajectory allows us to retain the core message of forgiveness and enemy love that is central to Matthew's Gospel, while still legitimately questioning the elements of vengeance and violence that seem to be particular to his editing of the Jesus-story.

TRANSFERRING OUR VIOLENCE TO GOD

As previously discussed, the New Testament authors were introducing the idea of forgiveness and enemy love in the context of a socio-religious culture steeped in the assumption that justice could only come about through violence. So while we may rightfully flinch at some of the vindictive sentiments expressed in Matthew, his original readers would likely not have, just as they would not have questioned the institution of slavery.

Indeed, it is safe to assume that Matthew and his community saw these violent descriptions positively, (perhaps comparable to how we regard the violent scenes in action movies positively), otherwise Matthew would not have added them in. So even as we recognize that the other three Evangelists seem to have taken a different course from Matthew in regards to a violent picture of God's judgment and character, the place to start in trying to understand Matthew's additions is to ask how this may have been regarded as positive within Matthew's community. What might have been the appeal?

Many scholars have suggested that Matthew's focus on violent apocalyptic language may have been a way of dealing with persecution, hypothesizing that Matthew and his community took comfort in thinking that while they were called to forego retaliation, God would one day avenge them. Thus the hope of God's future judgment may have enabled them to remain committed to nonviolence in the face of enduring violence and suffering.

While we of course cannot really know if this was the case, we do know that many others since then have expressed such sentiments in the face of suffering violence. A contemporary example of this perspective is Miroslav Volf who argues in his book *Exclusion and Embrace* that the only way to sustain a commitment to nonviolence in a violent world is not by relinquishing our desire for retribution and violence, but instead by *deferring* and *transferring* these to God:

> Without entrusting oneself to the God who judges justly, it will hardly be possible to follow the crucified messiah and refuse to retaliate when abused. The certainty of God's just judgment at the end of history is the presupposition for the renunciation of violence in the middle of it.[88]

In other words, according to Volf, the violent image of God contained in Matthew is a necessary part of Matthew's message of nonviolence. As Volf puts it, "The practice of nonviolence requires a belief in divine vengeance."[89] Volf says this in the context of the ethnic cleansing of the Yugoslav wars that ravaged his home country. Thus Volf writes this challenge to those who are inclined to reject his thesis:

---

88 Miroslav Volf,. *Exclusion and Embrace: A Theological Exploration of Identity, Otherness, and Reconciliation* (Nashville: Abindon Press, 1996), 302.

89 Volf, *Exclusion*, 304.

I suggest imagining that you are delivering a lecture in a war zone ... Among your listeners are people whose cities and villages have been first plundered, then burned and leveled to the ground, whose daughters and sisters have been raped, whose fathers and brothers have had their throats slit. The topic of the lecture: A Christian attitude towards violence. The thesis: we should not retaliate since God is perfect noncoercive love. Soon you would discover that it takes the quiet of a suburban home for the birth of the thesis that human nonviolence corresponds to God's refusal to judge. In a scorched land, soaked in the blood of the innocent, it will invariably die.[90]

It is hard not to hear the pain behind Volf's words. I do not imagine that I can comprehend the suffering and loss that he or others who have endured the horrors of war have undergone. However, I do believe that there is a better message that we could give to those in that war torn land than the hope of divine retaliation.

Certainly, people should not be expected to sit passively in the face of abuse, but that does not mean that their only other options are either immediate violent retribution or deferred and transferred retribution. There is the very real possibility of restorative and healing action here and now—involving both victims and perpetrators. This is something we can and must take part in.

---

90   Volf, *Exclusion*, 304.

As discussed in the previous chapter, nonviolence should not be understood as passive *inaction*. While Volf laudably embraces nonviolence and argues against retaliation, the difficulty is that he seems to view nonviolence precisely as a kind of inaction. He describes God's action in the world as one of patiently waiting for evildoers to repent, and complains that "every day of patience in a world of violence means more violence ... waiting for evildoers to reform means letting suffering continue."[91] Consequently, Volf concludes that, in a world of violence, if God did not "wield the sword ... God would not be worthy of our worship."[92] His assumption here is that the only two possibilities are *either God's violence or God's passive inaction*. Love in itself is "impotent," he says, to those who have made themselves "immune" to its lure.[93]

The issue this raises is how one is "lured" into repentance. Is it simply by God patiently waiting? What causes a hurtful person to care? Volf is correct that simply waiting is an ineffective means. Likewise, force is equally ineffective. Like it or not, you simply cannot coerce someone into being loving. It is simply not possible to force a person to show empathy. Regardless of how much violence or force we were willing to exert, the result would be to make a person worse, not better.

So what *does* make a person better? As we've seen in the previous chapter, while both force and passivity do not work,

---

91 Volf, *Exclusion,* 299–300.

92 Volf, *Exclusion,* 303.

93 Volf, *Exclusion,* 298.

what has been found to work is restorative justice—specifically, working with people to develop empathy and self-reflection, which in turn, changes their perception of their world around them, their awareness of themselves and others, and in turn their ability to navigate interpersonal conflict in socially appropriate ways rather than resorting to violence.

In the RSVP program, discussed in the previous chapter, we learned how this kind of active engagement with violent criminals enabled them to develop self-reflection and empathy, turning people who had formerly been "immune" to love, as Volf puts it, and helping them to become self-reflective, taking responsibility for the harm they had done, developing empathy and healthy coping skills, and thereby reversing the pattern of violence that had previously shaped their lives.

This demonstrates that it is possible to change the minds and wills of abusive people in a nonviolent and non-coercive way. It does this with the most vile and violent people in our society, and has been documented to be deeply effective at reducing the rate of recidivism, where the usual punitive means of our prison systems have dramatically failed to do so.

So I ask: If we puny humans can do that, cannot God all the more so? Is God less good or less capable than we are? Would not God's worthiness be better demonstrated in overcoming evil with good, rather than in enacting future vengeance?

If the hope of God's future retaliation on our behalf can help people to cope with their own feelings of hurt in the face of being wronged, allowing them to restrain themselves from being pulled into the self-perpetuating cycles of revenge, then this can be regarded as a positive move in the right direction.

We might view this as a sort of "harm reduction" technique, similar to those used to help people struggling with drug addiction. This can be a good place to start, a crucial first step out of a world that still sacralizes retribution as a virtue. However, we can and should be willing to move beyond this point, when we have better possibilities before us—possibilities that are not merely theoretical, but demonstrably effective in the real world. Working with victims of violence to help them to recover—which is the central focus of restorative justice—most certainly is needed in a war torn land. What has no place is the proclamation of passivity in the face of evil.

AN APOCALYPTIC OF PEACE

Coming full circle, let's take the above contemporary example of Volf and tie it back into Matthew's Gospel. Volf's main focus is to argue against violence, to find a way to maintain a commitment to nonviolence in a violent world. Likewise, the central focus of Matthew's Gospel is one of radical forgiveness and enemy love.

This nonviolent emphasis is critical to keep in perspective. If the intent of Matthew's additions of apocalyptic language emphasizing God's judgment were—similar to Volf's—a way of enabling people to embrace nonviolence by transferring their desire for retribution to God, then we can view this sympathetically as a positive first step on the path out of the vicious cycle of retaliatory violence. It is an appeal that speaks to people who feel a need for vengeance, beginning there, and pulling them in the direction of nonviolence and peace.

I would therefore propose that Matthew has added apocalyptic language to the parables of Jesus with the intent of tapping into the hopes of the Jewish people for liberation from bondage. Apocalyptic literature uses vivid symbolism to describe the spiritual significance of real world events. In particular, Jewish apocalyptic was intended to give hope to those who were suffering and oppressed, looking forward to a return from exile where Israel would be restored and their enemies destroyed.

Consequently, for his Jewish audience, familiar with this genre, the apocalyptic language used by Matthew would not have evoked visions of hell and eternal torment, but instead would have reminded them of the long awaited promise of a return from exile, which was commonly understood to be accomplished by military victory led by the messiah warrior-king who would vanquish Israel's oppressors and restore justice.

Jewish apocalyptic taps into these expectations employing violent imagery and descriptions of vengeance. This was the violent hope of his religious audience. This was the starting point of Matthew's audience, just as the starting point of Volf's audience is our own culture's pervasive assumption that the only way to bring about justice is through violence.[94]

That is the starting point where Matthew's religious audience begins, but it is not where Matthew leaves them. Matthew has added a twist to the typical apocalyptic expectation: Rather than taking up the sword—which was the means by which "salvation" continually came about in the Old Testament, both in the historical books and in the Prophets—Matthew instead proclaims that faithfulness to Torah is exhibited by practicing complete nonviolence, forgiving rather than retaliating.

This entails a radical break from the assumptions of his own religious heritage, not to mention the assumption of Rome. The way they would demonstrate their righteousness in the middle of a sinful world, and thus escape the coming judgment, was not by being zealous in battle as Joshua, Phinehas, or the Maccabees had, but by demonstrating Christ's way of enemy love.

---

94 It is impossible to speak of apocalyptic in the New Testament without mentioning Revelation, which likewise has been singled out for its focus on violent descriptions of God's final judgment. A growing number of scholars and theologians however have made the case that Revelation's use of apocalyptic should in fact be read nonviolently —similar in many ways to the reading of Matthew's use of apocalyptic that I am presenting here. For a good short introduction to the issues involved see Richard Hays *The Moral Vision of the New Testament* (San Francisco: HarperSanFrancisco, 1996), 169–185; David J. Neville, "Faithful, True, Violent? Christology and 'Divine Vengeance' in the Revelation of John" *Compassionate Eschatology: The Future as Friend* (Eugene, Or.: Cascade, 2011); Thomas R. Yoder Neufeld, *Killing Enmity: Violence and the New Testament* (Grand Rapids: Baker, 2011), 122–135. For more in depth treatments, see Michael J. Gorman, *Reading Revelation Responsibly: Uncivil Worship and Witness: Following the Lamb into the New Creation* (Eugene, Or.: Cascade, 2011); J. Nelson Kraybill, *Apocalypse and Allegiance: Worship, Politics and Devotion in the Book of Revelation* (Brazos, 2010).

Matthew is beginning with the assumptions of his ancient Jewish audience—an oppressed people longing for judgment and retribution. Appealing to their longing for retributive justice through the use of the familiar apocalyptic language, Matthew then makes a huge reversal in combining these apocalyptic visions with the gospel's core message of enemy love— completely excluding human participation in violence, leaving this in God's hands.

Just as Jesus begins his parables in the familiar thought-world of his audience (where slavery, kings, and torture were normal parts of the scenery), and then pushes a counter-cultural kingdom concept—so too, Matthew begins with familiar apocalyptic language which expressed an oppressed people's hope for violent retribution, and uses this to urge people steeped in that violent hope to instead renounce the way of violence.

Putting Things in Perspective

A typical flat reading of the Bible would insist that regardless of what we might think, we need to unquestioningly take what Matthew says about God here as the final authoritative word on the matter. A major problem with this, as we have seen, is that this approach has led Christians over the centuries to use the Bible to justify things like slavery and child abuse. That should give us pause. A better approach, I would suggest, is to read this as representing a point along the trajectory set by Christ.

Just as we find in the New Testament a less-than-ultimate view of slavery, we likewise find in places a less-than-ultimate view of God. Seeing this as the first steps along a trajectory, we can appreciate the bold move expressed in the New Testament's unanimous rejection of human participation in violence in God's name, while at the same time recognizing that their application of Christ's revelation of God's true nature needs to faithfully be taken further by us today—abolishing slavery, ending child abuse, finding better ways to deal with crime and international conflict, and finally in understanding that God's true nature is revealed in Christlike enemy love, not in violent retribution.

With that said, it is important to keep in perspective that while I believe that Matthew (and Miroslav Volf) are wrong to project a desire for violent retribution onto God, they are still, in their core message of renunciation of violence, far further along than we are as a nation.

Looking at how our country in particular and Western culture as a whole responds to those we regard as criminals and terrorists —in other words, how we treat those we regard as our enemies— it is clear that we do not love our enemies. On the contrary, our government still tortures and kills its enemies, and claims to do so in the name of justice.

So while we may criticize Matthew for not going further in allowing his understanding of Christ's example of enemy love to shape his understanding of God's true nature as revealed in Christ, the sobering fact is: We have yet to take that first step of enemy love ourselves as a society some two thousand years later.

My criticism of Matthew and Volf is therefore a disagreement among those who are ultimately working towards the same end. Honestly, I wish I lived in the world Matthew imagined, where no Christian participated in killing people, and all of our lives were characterized by forgiveness and care for the least.

That is Matthew's portrait of the way of Jesus, and if the price for that were adopting a wrong conception of God's future retribution, then I would be more than happy to lose that argument. Because, in the end, what really matters is how we treat each other. For my part, I am perfectly content to trust God to judge rightly so long as we humans stop hurting each other in God's name or in the name of justice.

The bottom line here is that while we can find disagreement among the New Testament authors as to God's violence, the New Testament is unanimous in its radical rejection of human participation in violence. That is, quite literally, a matter of life and death importance.

CHAPTER 10

RE-THINKING
BIBLICAL AUTHORITY

The trajectory reading presented over these last several chapters raises some pretty big questions about the authority and inspiration of Scripture. If there are things endorsed in the Bible like genocide or slavery which we can and must clearly recognize as wrong, then in what sense can we say that the Bible is inspired, let alone infallible or inerrant?

The terms inerrant and infallible are often times confused since the two words in their common English usage are virtually synonymous. However, as theological terms they differ significantly. Inerrancy refers to the Bible being free from *error*. Infallibility on the other hand refers to the Bible not *failing* (from the Latin *fallere*, literally "cause to fall" or figuratively "fail, be lacking or defective") which stresses that the Bible is a trustworthy guide that we can fully rely on in all matters to which it speaks.

Those who affirm the Bible's inerrancy also affirm its infallibility and stress that Scripture cannot be infallible (a reliable guide) if it is not also completely error free (inerrant). Others, recognizing the many scientific and scribal errors in the Bible, maintain that the Bible, while not being inerrant, is nevertheless infallible. That is, it is a trustworthy guide that we can fully rely on in matters of faith, doctrine, and morality.

A major problem with both the ideas of inerrancy and infallibility is that we humans are not free from error and failing ourselves. So even if we begin with the assumption of an inerrant or infallible Bible, by the time the manuscripts are translated into another language and culture, and then read by people who themselves are fallible and liable to error like us, there are so many levels of potential misunderstanding that the idea of Scripture being inerrant or infallible becomes rather moot. Even if the Bible is infallible, we are not.

The fact that there are so many conflicting interpretations of the Bible—even among those who view the Bible as inerrant and infallible—makes this conclusion unavoidable. Christian Smith refers to this as the problem of *pervasive interpretive pluralism* meaning that it is simply an undeniable empirical fact that evangelicals have consistently disagreed with each other as to what Scripture teaches.[95] In other words, it is does not make much sense to claim that the Bible is an unfailing guide in what it says if we cannot agree on what it says. An easy example of this can be found by doing a search on Amazon.com for "four views" which results in page after page of books with titles like these:

Four Views on Hell
Four Views of the End Times
Four Views on Divine Providence
Four Views on Salvation in a Pluralistic World
Four Views on the Apostle Paul
The Nature of the Atonement: Four Views
Four Views on Eternal Security.[96]

These books, and the many others like them, address major topics like hell, the atonement, salvation, divorce, war, and so on. In each we find multiple opposing views where each proponent is convinced that *their* particular interpretation of the Bible is the correct one. So if those who affirm that the Bible is infallible in

---

95   Christian Smith, *The Bible Made Impossible: Why Biblicism Is Not a Truly Evangelical Reading of Scripture* (Grand Rapids: Brazos, 2012).

96   For a longer list, see Smith, *The Bible Made Impossible,* 22–23.

what it teaches can't agree on what exactly it is that the Bible in fact teaches—at times vehemently disagreeing—how then can we practically say that the Bible is our "supreme and final authority" on these matters? As Christian Smith cogently observes:

> The "biblicism" that pervades much of American evangelicalism is untenable and needs to be abandoned in favor of a better approach to Christian truth and authority. By untenable I do not simply mean that it is wrong, but rather that it is literally impossible, at least when attempted consistently on its own terms. It cannot actually be sustained, practiced, and defended. Biblicism is one kind of an attempt to explain and act on the authority of the Bible, but it is a misguided one. In the end it cannot and in fact does not work.[97]

In other words, the fact that people cannot agree on what the Bible says means that entire concept of infallibility—meaning the belief that it is not possible to be misled by the Bible—simply does not work in practice.

It gets worse. As I have argued in this book, the problem is not simply that people cannot agree on what the Bible says, but that the Bible—when it is interpreted in an unquestioning way—inevitably leads to violence and abuse. In other words, when there are no means by which to evaluate which interpretations are good and which are hurtful because of an a priori assumption that the Bible overrides conscience, the inevitable

---

97 Smith, *The Bible Made Impossible*, 3.

result of pervasive interpretive pluralism is that *some* of those interpretations will be abusive.

Just as it is an empirical fact that evangelicals can't seem to agree on what the "clear meaning" of Scripture is, it is equally an empirical historical fact that an unquestioning reading of the Bible has a long history of people endorsing things like slavery, child abuse, and genocide—all in the name of an "infallible" Bible. To read the Bible in an unquestioning way invariably leads to acts of violence and abuse.

This constitutes a much more substantial criticism of inerrancy and infallibility than the typical focus on scribal errors. In comparison, scribal errors seem rather trivial. After all, this book very likely contains some typos too! There's an enormous difference, however, between a typo and inciting people to commit acts of violence in God's name.

The simple fact of history is that biblicism's unquestioning way of reading the Bible ends up fueling and legitimizing violence and abuse, and does so precisely because we have been persistently taught to believe that biblical commands override conscience. As morally responsible adults, we need to recognize the moral bankruptcy inherent in the narrative of *unquestioning obedience* and its contemporary expression in authoritarian biblicism, and instead adopt a better way of reading the Bible modeled after Jesus and his way of *faithful questioning* motivated by compassion.

233

THE CENTRALITY OF EXPERIENCE IN SCRIPTURE

Inerrancy and infallibility simply do not work as a way to safeguard against error, and in fact because an authoritarianism reading overrides conscience and thought, abuse becomes the inevitable result. To read the Bible in an authoritarian unquestioning way is to read it immorally.

In contrast, the trajectory approach proposed here embraces faithful questioning as essential. This trajectory reading works by adopting Jesus' method of "looking at the fruits" of a particular interpretation or teaching—evaluating the evidence of its observable effects in life as to whether they result in flourishing or harm, peace or devastation.

For example, based on observable evidence we know that child abuse and slavery are deeply harmful. This therefore leads us to re-assess how we may have read God as endorsing these in Scripture. If we recognize that a particular interpretation leads to observable harm, this necessarily means that we need to stop and reassess our course. To continue on a course we know to be harmful, simply because "the Bible says so" is morally irresponsible. The way of faithful questioning, of looking at the fruits, is how we can ensure that Scripture is read in such a way as to lead us to love. That involves our always seeking, always reforming, always growing in Christ-shaped love.

This is an approach to Scripture that is rooted in life, rather than rooted in a text. Scripture is not our master, Jesus is, and the role of Scripture is to serve a servant function leading us to Christ. Here experience is central, i.e. *the evidence of observable effects in life* is central in evaluating the merit of a particular reading as to whether we are reading it so as to lead us to love and life, which is the aim of Scripture.

Scripture is thus *inspired* in the sense that it acts as a sacrament —as a window through which we can encounter God's love, through which the Spirit can communicate with us, loving us, correcting us, transforming our mind and heart into Christ-likeness. Scripture is thus not an end in itself (as if the goal were to simply read *about* Jesus, but not know him), rather it is a vehicle intended to bring us into loving communion with Christ.

It's about leading us to *experience*—about a lived faith, about loving relationship. This focus on life-based experience was central to how Jesus, Paul, and the Apostles interpreted Scripture. Let's take a look at that in a bit more detail.

JESUS AND EXPERIENCE: As we saw in chapter two, Jesus frequently challenged the Pharisees for their hurtful use of Scripture, and he did this based on *observing* the damaging effect this was having on people's lives. The Pharisees made sure to follow every letter of the law, but ignored how their reading of Scripture was wounding people, shutting them out from God's love and healing—in other words, they had a reading of Scripture detached from experience.

It is hard to over-emphasize how important this connection to experience was for Jesus. It mattered to him because he understood that when Scripture is read in a way that is detached from experience it has deeply hurtful results. Jesus goes so far as to call this an "unforgivable sin" and "blasphemy of the Holy Spirit."

Now, if you grew up evangelical as I did, you likely learned a very different understanding of what "blasphemy of the Holy Spirit" means. However, Jesus originally used this phrase in the context of the religious gatekeepers of his faith rejecting the work of the Spirit happening among them through his healing ministry because it conflicted with their understanding of Scripture.

Matthew tells us of a time Jesus healed a man who was blind and mute. The Pharisees object to his healing, saying that this was the work of the devil. Jesus in response says, "I tell you, every kind of sin and slander can be forgiven, but blasphemy against the Spirit will not be forgiven" (Matt 12:31). Blasphemy of the Holy Spirit here thus refers to their denying their *experience* of what they witnessed God's Spirit doing right there in front of them—healing, giving life, loving, setting free—denying this because it conflicted with their understanding of Scripture and with their tradition. Why is Jesus so opposed to this? Because they are shutting people out from God's love.

236

Now, let me say emphatically that I don't believe Jesus meant this sin was *literally* unforgivable. As we've seen, Jesus commonly used provocative and hyperbolic language to drive home his message. His point here—the importance of which he is underlining for us in the starkest of terms—is that it's deadly for us to get so stuck on laws and so-called "orthodoxy" that we miss what God is doing in our midst, that we miss out on love. As Jesus saw it, to place a priority on one's reading of the text *over the experience of what God was doing* was the greatest of sins.

Religion so often gets stuck exactly here, thinking we're defending "traditional values" or "historical faith" or "God's Word" when really what we are doing is missing God because we have missed compassion. The take-away for us here is that when we cling to hurtful interpretations of the Bible—ignoring common sense, ignoring the damaging effects it is having in people's lives, ignoring what the Spirit is doing right in front of us —this truly is blaspheming God's Spirit, because the result is that God's reputation is ruined by a stagnant and heartless religion and the deeply hurtful image of God this presents.

This all goes to underscore how central experience was to Jesus. As people heard the liberating words of Jesus, as they *experienced* healing and liberation in their lives as he touched and healed them, it was that direct *experience* of life that led them to follow. As James Dunn writes, Jesus observed God working through him and this experience likewise shaped how Jesus understood Scripture:

237

The power which he experienced working through his ministry was a power to heal, not to destroy ... his own experience of God, of divine power and inspiration, made clear to him what parts of the Old Testament prophecy were applicable to and descriptive of his ministry, *and what were not.*"[98]

In other words, the way that Jesus read Scripture was shaped by his own *direct experience* of God in his life. Jesus therefore understands his messianic mission to be radically different from what his fellow Jews were expecting. Jesus' experience of the Spirit shaped his understanding of Scripture, and not the other way around.

PAUL AND EXPERIENCE: This focus on lived experience was equally formative for Paul's understanding of Scripture. As we have seen, previous to his conversion, Paul had in fact read Scripture and arrived at a very different conclusion—aligning himself with a toxic narrative of violent zeal for purity. In other words, *Paul had read the Bible extensively, and gotten God completely wrong.* It wasn't until Paul was encountered by Jesus that he was able to go back and re-read Scripture in the light of Christ, consequently embracing a radically different narrative found in those same pages.

---

98 James D. G. Dunn, *Jesus and the Spirit* (Grand Rapids: Eerdmans, 1975), 61. Emphasis added.

Jesus' and Paul's direct *experience* of God's gracious restorative power in and through them was definitive in shaping how they read Scripture, and the narrative they subsequently embraced in its pages. This lived and experienced narrative of compassion and restoration became the key hermeneutical lens through which they now read the Bible. As we have seen, it determined which of the Old Testament narratives they embodied and emulated, and which ones they did not.

THE NEW TESTAMENT AND EXPERIENCE: The New Testament is a record of the disciples' encounter with Jesus, calling us to enter into that same encounter and relationship ourselves. The gospel proclamation is not about a mere intellectual assent to a doctrinal formulation. Rather, it tells the story of how in Jesus, God had come and dwelt among humanity, and in this relational encounter the disciples had found life. They were witnesses to this story, to this "good news," in order that we might encounter the same living Christ relationally as they had. John writes:

> This we proclaim concerning the Word of life … *We proclaim to you what we have seen and heard*, so that you also may have fellowship with us. And our fellowship is with the Father and with his Son, Jesus Christ. (1 John 1:1-4)

We can observe throughout the New Testament how Jesus' disciples interpreted the Bible in a new, and indeed subversive way, based on their experience of the Spirit of Christ. The

239

reason, for example, that we as Christians do not obey the food laws in the Old Testament today, as well as the reason why the early church decided to make the radical move to invite Gentiles into fellowship, was because of Peter and the other disciples' *experience* of the new thing God was doing in Jesus.

What changed Peter's mind was the Spirit speaking to him through a vision, coupled with his friendship with a foreigner named Cornelius who led Peter to exclaim, "You are well aware that it is against our law for a Jew to associate with or visit a Gentile. But God has shown me that I should not call anyone impure or unclean" (Acts 10:28).

In other words, the decision to include Gentiles in the faith was based on Peter's experience—observing what the Spirit was doing in their lives and the lives of those they had previously regarded as "unclean" that led to the disciples deciding to break with both the law of Moses and with centuries of religious tradition.

Again, notice here that Peter and the early church's basis for this was not based on a careful exegesis of Scripture (as Protestant theology would stress), nor was it based on following their religious tradition (as Catholic theology would). On the contrary, they were breaking with their previous understanding of Scripture, breaking with their religion, and breaking with centuries of tradition, and instead going with their experience, with what they observed the Spirit was doing.

The Science of Faith

Now, if you find all of this surprising, you would be in good company. This focus on experience as the primary evaluative criterion for theological praxis is pretty much the *exact opposite* of what you learn in seminary. If you're from a Wesleyan background you learn to evaluate doctrinal claims through the "quadrilateral" of *Scripture, reason, tradition and experience*. Scripture is seen as the primary source, balanced together with tradition, reason, and, last of all, experience.

Other traditions, who tend to distrust experience as a valid category for doctrinal reflection at all, elect to drop experience from the list entirely, thus adopting what's often referred to as the "three legged stool" of *Scripture, reason and tradition* as their sources of knowledge. So the priority is placed on Scripture, understood in the context of tradition and reason, with experience only coming in last, if at all.

What this means is that while for Jesus and the apostles experience was the primary category that trumped all others, experience has in contrast been given the lowest importance by later Christian theology—sometimes being disregarded altogether. In fact, experience has traditionally been disparaged by subsequent Christian theology as being based either on unreliable emotions or subjective individual experience.

It's true that our emotions are subjective, but so is our reason. In fact, *everything* we are involved in as humans is always limited, subjective, and fallible—including our interpretation of Scripture. So while our emotions are indeed subjective (as is every aspect of our humanity), they serve a valid and important place in our lives that should not simply be dismissed. To see this otherwise is to make the error of modernism which placed an over-emphasis on certainty based on reason.

That said, it is simply incorrect to think of experience exclusively in terms of emotions or private inner experience. The focus on experience, typical of Jesus and the Apostles, is more accurately understood as a focus on what they experienced in their lives and relationships together, *"We proclaim to you what we have seen and heard"* (1 John 1:3). That is, the stress was on our shared human experience, on observing how life works—how we work, rather than on something exclusively private and internal.

Observing life and how it works is of course the focus of both the natural and social sciences. A crucial aspect of the scientific method is that a hypothesis is developed and modified based on new evidence.

While the Apostles, being from a pre-scientific era, would of course not have formulated it in these terms, we can nevertheless recognize that when they modified their understanding of Scripture based on the new evidence of what they observed God doing in their lives, this in fact parallels (or we might say it foreshadows) the basic scientific method of modifying a hypothesis based on new experiential evidence.

Consequently, perhaps instead of referring to "experience" (which implies in the minds of many a stress on private emotions), it would more accurate and descriptive today to instead speak of *empirical evidence*—that is, knowledge acquired by means of observation.

Understanding "experience" in terms of empirical observation not only makes sense today, but is also reflective of the original use of the term within the Wesleyan Quadrilateral. Wesley's use of the "quadrilateral" was originally developed in the 18th century in the context of the dawning scientific revolution which was gaining wide influence at the time. The concept of "experience" (the term Wesley used was actually "experimental") is thus drawn directly from the scientific terminology of Wesley's day.[99] Today, what was then called "experimental" evidence, is now referred to in the sciences as "empirical evidence."

Since Wesley's time in the 1700s the sciences have of course developed much further, including the development of the social sciences which deal specifically with both inner experience as well as our shared human experience and relationships.

The bottom line here is that the concept of experience—both for the writers of the New Testament, and for Wesley—should not be understood primarily as a focus on private internal religious feelings, but more substantially refers to theology's connection to life, recognized in observable shared human experience. As Don Thorsten explains:

---

99 See Don Thorsten, *The Wesleyan Quadrilateral: Scripture, Tradition, Reason, & Experience as a Model of Evangelical Theology* (Lexington: Emeth Press, 2005).

> [Wesley] was primarily concerned with the intuitive experience of transcendent reality of the Holy Spirit in a person's life. But because such experiences are to a certain extent empirically understandable and observable, Wesley was willing to investigate seriously the relevance of religious experience to the formulation of theology. He wished to present his theological work in a way that was consonant with the best in contemporary scientific investigation rather than contrary to it.[100]

Today we of course know vastly more about human psychology than Wesley possibly could have. I would therefore suggest in light of this that theology must expand its focus beyond strictly "religious" experiences to include all human relational experience. This would include listening to insights from the social sciences.

One example of this would be recognizing the psychological damage resulting from physical abuse of children and allowing this to change our approach to child rearing. In other words, a focus of Jesus' method of evaluating "the fruits" of a particular interpretation and application of Scripture needs to be one that looks to the *observable effects in people's lives*—including observable effects on a person's personality and emotions. If we can see that the application of a particular interpretation leads to observable harm, then we need to stop and reassess our course.

---

100 Thorsten, *The Wesleyan Quadrilateral*, 30.

Note that the measure of "right" interpretation here is not based primarily on evaluating whether the text has been properly understood (the question of proper exegesis), but on evaluating the *results* when it is applied in our lives—observing whether it results in bringing about life or death, flourishing or harm. As we have seen, Jesus saw the primary role and telos of Scripture as leading us to love. If we wish to read the Bible with that same aim, the question we need to ask is therefore not so much "Have I read this right?" but more importantly "Does this reading lead to life?"

This does not mean that one needs to be a scientist or scholar to read the Bible. It simply means that if we see that our interpretation is leading to hurt and not love then something is not right, and we need to pay attention to that. It means that if our conscience is telling us loudly "this feels really wrong" then that just might be the Holy Spirit speaking to us, and we need to listen.

Again, the problem is not that we don't know right from wrong, that we can't recognize hurt. The problem is that we've been taught to read the Bible in a way that shuts down thought and ignores our conscience. Reading in this way makes us less moral, and that's the exact opposite of what the Bible is supposed to do.

Let me be perfectly clear that I am by no means suggesting that the approach proposed above will lead us to the one "right" universal answer of what is good and right. There are many different ways humans can flourish. What I am proposing is something much more modest and basic: We should not turn off our brains or sear our consciences—as if doing so were what it means to be faithful to the Bible. That is precisely what a biblicist reading of Scripture does, and—as we have seen with the examples of both slavery and child abuse—the disastrous fruits of this throughout history are clear to see.

We as humans are not infallible. But for precisely this reason we need to continue to seek and continue to question. This is foundational to the scientific method itself which does not claim to have all the answers, but rather operates by a methodology that continually seeks to grow and ask and look. It is good to think. It is good to question in the name of compassion. It is good to have a morality rooted in life and our shared human experience. These are essential elements of a healthy faith.

Science is about observing how life works, and that's what we need to be doing, too. Science is not about clinging to a theory from the past, but rather is about always moving forward to deeper and better discoveries. Isaac Newton advances an understanding of physics, but then later that theory is changed with the discoveries of Einstein, and then later quantum physics. It would be silly to imagine that Isaac Newton would have been upset that Einstein's theory went beyond the confines of Newtonian physics.

In fact, Newton famously said, "If I have seen further it is only by standing on the shoulders of giants." In that same way, Einstein was able to get where he did by standing on the shoulders of people before him like Newton. The whole spirit of science is to welcome progress, not to restrict it. It does not cling to the past, but moves forward, building from the past.

Similarly, Scripture should not be read in a way that it tethers us to some frozen-in-time view from the past that we unquestionably apply now even though we can see it conflicts with what we understand about life, even though we can see that our reading leads to harm. Rather it must be read in a way that allows us to grow and build upon what Jesus taught. As Jesus says, "Very truly I tell you, whoever believes in me will do the works I have been doing, *and they will do even greater things than these*" (John 14:12).

All of this is to say that our reading of Scripture cannot be detached from life. Our interpretations cannot callously ignore the hurtful effects they have in people's lives. On the contrary, they should lead us to life, to abundant life, and more concretely *Scripture should lead us to the one who is Life.*

TRADITION AS COMMUNITY NOT AUTHORITY

The bottom line here is a vital connection to *life*. We need a way of reading Scripture rooted in life, not detached from it. This focus on experience needs to be understood in the context of a focus on *relationships* with God and others. This puts the stress on

247

a lived faith, connected to life and love. This relational emphasis underscores that the interpretive task needs to be done together in community, in relationship, rather than in isolation. This is commonly referred to as the role of "tradition" (also a part of the Wesleyan Quadrilateral), but the question we need to immediately ask here is: *What tradition?*

As we all know, Christian tradition has taken some pretty horrible turns over the years—burning people at the stake, holy wars, torture, and so on. So the last thing we need is an authoritarian tradition that claims to hold the keys to the truth and silences dissent through threat and exclusion. What we do need however, is *each other.*

Simply put, we need to hang out with people who are living out the way of grace, compassion, and enemy love. We need to interpret Scripture in community with others who are really living it, as well as hearing from those who in the past have walked the same narrow road we are now on. In other words, *we need to be connected to a Jesus-following tradition*—learning from the wisdom of those who have walked that way before us, demonstrating with their lives a sophisticated vision of what the way of Jesus looks like in practice.

Finally, a focus on experience emphasizes the need for a personal *lived* faith. We cannot truly know something until we experience it. Scripture is intended to lead us into a living, loving, life-changing relationship with the one who is Life, who is Love. Not just as a one-time encounter, but as a lifelong relationship where we know God's love and the experience of that love spills over into everything we do, so we show others the same love and mercy we have known.

For some, this will be experienced more directly by encountering God's love and grace through prayer, worship, and personal devotion. For many others this will be experienced primarily through the love of another person. Regardless of the way we experience this love, regardless of the way we encounter grace, the result is the same: When we experience how God can take broken things and make them beautiful and whole again— not only in our own lives, but also how we can become instruments of that kind of transformation in other people's lives, as well—this experience changes us, it converts us, it makes us thirst for more.

Anabaptists refer to this as the "hermeneutics of obedience" meaning that you can only properly interpret the Bible when you are *living* it. Through this relational formation—not only studying the words of Jesus, but *living* them, letting them become the air we breathe—we learn to practically recognize what reflects Christ and his way. We grow to have the "mind of Christ," as Paul says.

Such a lived experience of Christ's way of grace, compassion, and enemy love is absolutely essential to proper theology, and to the interpretation of Scripture. We need to come to the text as those who know grace and have been transformed by it. Otherwise, we are likely to miss Scripture's central point, which is

249

to point us to Christ, learning to love like he does, even as we are loved by him.

THE INSPIRATION OF THE HOLY SPIRIT

The aim of Scripture, as Jesus saw it, is to lead us to love. Reading on a trajectory therefore entails looking at the fruits that our interpretation and application of Scripture has in people's lives, evaluating its observable effects as to whether this leads to harm or to love. Looking at the fruits of the doctrines of inerrancy and infallibility we can see that, not only are they simply untenable, they also have a long history of leading people to override thought and conscience, justifying profound harm and violence.

How can we still say that Scripture is inspired when it can lead to such hurt and damage? All good things can become hurtful. Families are good things, intended to be safe and loving environments where we learn to love ourselves and others. However, when twisted by sin, families can be profoundly damaging and abusive, leaving lifelong scars. Likewise, Scripture is also good, intended to lead us to love. However—as we have seen—it, too, can be read in an abusive way. As Paul writes, "I found that the very commandment that was intended to bring life actually brought death" (Rom 7:10).

250

In this context, the inspiration of Scripture involves recognizing the Bible is not an end in itself, but a vehicle intended to lead us to a life-giving encounter with God's grace. The word "inspired" literally means in-Spirit-ed, that is, to be *indwelt* with the Spirit. We thus recognize that the Bible is inspired by God when it leads us to an encounter with the Spirit of God in Christ—when it leads us to love.

Scripture is *inspired* through God's active *illumination* of the text, breathing life into the page and revealing its truth to our hearts. "The letter kills," Paul writes, "but the Spirit gives life" (2 Cor 3:3). That is, apart from the illuminating work of the Spirit of Christ in the text, the Bible, Paul says, is a dead book, but through the living Spirit of God the text can come alive, pointing us to Christ. The text *alone* is not inspired apart from the Spirit. Rather, it *becomes* inspired (in-Spirit-ed) as the *rema* word of God breathes life into Scripture so that it becomes a sacrament for us where we can encounter the living God.

This view of the inspiration of Scripture is nothing new or novel. As Stanley Grenz documents, it is a perspective that was common throughout 18th century evangelicalism, which Grenz describes as "an evangelicalism that looked to Scripture as the vehicle through which the Spirit worked the miracles of salvation and sanctification. Sparked by their experience of the nurturing work of the Spirit through the pages of the Bible, evangelicals' overriding aim was to allow the message of the Bible to penetrate

251

into human hearts and to encourage the devotional use of the Bible."[101]

In contrast to this, Grenz explains that the biblicist understanding commonly held today among conservative evangelicals arose out of fundamentalism's reaction against modernism. As Grenz puts it, this shift from 18th century evangelical piety to modernist fundamentalism (and later Calvinist conservative evangelicalism),

> had the effect of transforming the ethos of the theological tradition of the purveyors of conservative piety from that of a gospel-focused endeavor that viewed the Bible as the vehicle of the Spirit's working to that of a Bible-focused task intent on maintaining the gospel of biblical orthodoxy.[102]

This shift, from a *gospel-focus* to a *book-focus,* is precisely why Christian Smith argues that modern biblicism is not a truly evangelical reading of Scripture.[103] In order to be truly *evangelical* our reading of Scripture needs to regain this gospel-focus.

Scripture is primary not because we find in it a collection of timeless truths that should be unquestioningly applied to our lives. This leads to promoting slavery and many other deeply

---

101 Stanley Grenz, *Renewing the Center: Evangelical Theology in a Post-Theological Era* (Grand Rapids: Baker Academic, 2000), 72–73.

102 Grenz, *Renewing the Center,* 92.

103 This point is made in the subtitle to Smith's book *Why Biblicism is Not a Truly Evangelical Reading of Scripture,* and discussed in the book's concluding section "Towards a Truly Evangelical Reading of Scripture." Smith, *The Bible Made Impossible,* 93 ff.

hurtful and immoral things in God's name. Yes, Scripture does contain many timeless truths, such as forgiveness, grace, enemy love, but we need to apply these with reflection and care. As we have seen, even these when applied in an unquestioning way can become hurtful.

Our reading of Scripture needs to be connected to life, and that begins with our connection to the one who is Life. The reason Scripture is primary is therefore first and foremost because it introduces us to Jesus. When John writes, "We proclaim to you what we have seen and heard, so that you also may have fellowship with us. And our fellowship is with the Father and with his Son, Jesus Christ" (1 John 1:1-4) what he is essentially saying is, "We met this guy Jesus, and want you to meet him, too!"

That's the primary purpose of Scripture, to lead us to the one who is Life, Love, Truth, and the Way. Scripture has the primary task of leading us into a living relationship with God in Christ, and then after that continuing to be a window through which we can commune with God, in which the Spirit can communicate God's love to us, leading us to love others with that same Jesus-shaped love. That's the devotional, Spirit-centered, gospel-focused reading that needs to be at the center of how we read Scripture *as Scripture.*

This gospel-focus begins in our experience of love and continues in a life of love. This connection to love is vital. As we grow in Christ's love we grow to share in Jesus' concern for those on the margins, those regarded as "least" and as "enemies" by

253

the religious leaders of his day, showing that same concern for those in our day who are marginalized, scapegoated by the religious leaders of our day. This is what led gospel-focused evangelicals in the 18th and 19th centuries to be at the forefront of social justice, caring for the poor, woman's rights, and the abolition of slavery.[104]

This *gospel-focus* is the opposite of the *book-focus* that has characterized the rise of fundamentalism at the beginning of the 20th century which was born as an embattled movement, and which now has come to characterize that same embattled stance in conservative evangelicalism, particularly through the influence of what is known as the *Neo-Reformed* movement.

This is a belligerent movement which places its priority on defending a book, defending doctrine, regardless of how much this hurts people. Anyone who draws attention to this hurt is subsequently cast as "outside" and regarded as a threat. The priority is not on caring for people, and in particular the least and enemies, rather the priority is placed on defending a book. Consequently, to the extent that evangelicalism has been shaped by this angry antagonistic *book-focused* Neo-Reformed theology, it has come to mirror the Phariseeism that Jesus so adamantly opposed.

The Bible was never meant to be a substitute for that living relationship with God. On the contrary, it's meant to lead us into that life-giving relationship. Scripture needs to lead us *into* this

---

104 Donald Dayton, *Discovering an Evangelical Heritage* (Grand Rapids, Baker Academic, 1988).

lived experience of the power of the gospel—causing our lives to be shaped by the gospel, so the gospel story becomes *our* story.

If we wish to regain this truly *evangelical* gospel-focus, we need to move from trusting in a book to trusting in Christ. Our foundation is therefore not in an allegedly infallible Bible (which is an illusion since we are not infallible in our interpretations). Rather, our foundation is in the risen Christ, who the Bible is meant to point us to.

"You study the Scriptures diligently because you think that in them you have eternal life," Jesus says, "These are the very Scriptures that testify about me" (John 5:39). Paul describes a "veil," similar to the one Moses wore over his face, covering the law, preventing it from reflecting God, and declares that this veil "has not been removed, because only in Christ is it taken away" (2 Cor 3:14). The Bible is a witness to that relational self-disclosure of God in history, with the primary goal not of being a collection of doctrinal propositions about God, but in encountering us relationally with the living God in Christ. "Christ is the goal of the law" Paul writes (Rom 10:4, CEB). Scripture is therefore not an end in itself, but points us to that life-giving relationship, leading us into a life of Christ-like love.

Martin Luther thus describes the Bible as the manger in which Christ is found. Without the manger you will not find Christ, but you dare not confuse Christ with the manger. We love the Bible because through it we encounter Jesus, but we do not have a relationship with a book, but with the living Word, Jesus Christ.

The gospel is thus bigger than any book, and bigger than us, too. Our faith does not rest in a book, but in the eternal Logos of God, the true Word that existed before a single word was ever written, and to whom all Scripture points. Truth is not found in a book, but in the one who says, "I am the way, the truth, and the life" (John 14:6).

That means Truth (with a capital T) is not abstract and static, cataloged in a collection of eternal unchanging propositions. Truth is a *Someone*. Truth is personal and alive. The teleological aim of Scripture is to bring us into a living relationship with the Logos of God, Jesus Christ. Our faith is anchored in the living Christ, not in a book.

That means we indeed have a sure foundation, but not one built on our having the truth, but rather in the one who is "the Truth" having us.

We cannot claim to have a monopoly on truth. The best we can hope for is to let truth have a monopoly on us, and the way we do that is by living in openness to the one who is Truth. Our faith is not held up by our perfect formulations or in anything we do. Rather, it is God who holds us up even in our weakness and dependency.

Now, someone might legitimately ask: "How can we then know that our interpretation of Jesus is right? How can we be sure we aren't reading the Bible wrong?" The simple answer is:

We can't.

We are humans and so we will inevitably get things wrong, even with the very best of intentions and hearts open to the Spirit, even as part of a Jesus-following community.

As adults, this is simply a fact of life that we need to have the maturity and courage to face head-on. That's why we need to have a faith that can ask those hard questions—including questioning ourselves. That's why we need to have a way of reading Scripture characterized by humility and seeking. That's why we need to make room in our communities for honest questions—not seeing these as a problem to get past, but as the mark of a healthy faith.

This will thus involve a constant journey of growing and stretching and questioning because interpreting the Bible aright is ultimately a matter of discipleship—a matter of seeking, learning and growing.

In the end, the real problem of violence in the Bible is not so much the particular passages that seem to endorse it, but more significantly a particular way of reading Scripture that shuts down all questioning and conscience. John Collins writes:

> The Bible has contributed to violence in the world precisely because it has been taken to confer a degree of certitude that transcends human discussion and argumentation. Perhaps the most constructive thing a biblical critic can do toward lessening the contribution of the Bible to violence in the world is to show that such certitude is an illusion.[105]

---

105 John J. Collins, *Does the Bible Justify Violence* (Minneapolis: Fortress, 2004), 32–33.

We might wish that we could simply blindly trust in the authority of the Bible, and that this could keep us safe and secure. But as Collins says, that certainty is an illusion, and a dangerous one at that.

The witness of history demonstrates, time and time again, that rather than making us "safe," this unquestioning way of reading Scripture puts us on a certain path to violence and bloodshed. As Pascal has said, "Men never do evil so completely and cheerfully as when they do it from religious conviction."[106]

Uncertainty is therefore not something to be feared. It's quite the other way around: Uncertainty and questioning are virtues to be embraced, because it is precisely our *not* being certain that keeps us all safe, and it is faithful questioning that moves us forward.

Questioning and struggling are therefore not signs of weakness, they are signs of a healthy and mature faith. Learning to read the Bible like Jesus did means being empowered to faithfully question in the name of compassion. It likewise means learning to read the Bible as morally responsible adults, aware of our own limitations. Because in the final analysis, faith is not about certainty; faith is about humility and trust.

---

106 Blaise Pascal, *Pensées* (#894) in W. F. Trotter (Tr), *Pensées / The Provincial Letters* (New York: Random House, 1941), 314.

BIBLIOGRAPHY

Brueggemann, Walter. Theology of the Old Testament: Testimony, Dispute, Advocacy. Minneapolis: Fortress, 2005.

Cavey, Bruxy. The End of Religion: Encountering the Subversive Spirituality of Jesus. Colorado Springs: NavPress, 2007.

Collins, John J. Does the Bible Justify Violence? Minneapolis: Fortress, 2004.

_____. "The Zeal of Phinehas: The Bible and the Legitimation of Violence" JBL 122/1 (2003) 3-21.

Davies, Eryl W. The Immoral Bible: Approaches to Biblical Ethics. New York: T&T Clark, 2010.

_____. "The Morally Dubious Passages of the Hebrew Bible," Currents in Biblical Research 3.2 (April 2005) 197-228. 220.

Dawkins, Richard. The God Delusion. New York: Houghton Mifflin Harcourt, 2006.

Dayton, Donald. Discovering an Evangelical Heritage. Grand Rapids, Baker Academic, 1988.

Dever, Wiliam G. Who Were the Early Israelites, and Where Did They Come From? Grand Rapids: Wm. B. Eerdmans Publishing, 2003.

Driscoll, Mark. "7 Big Questions." Relevant Magazine #24 (Jan/Feb 2007). http://web.archive.org/web/20071013102203/http://rele vantmagazine.com/god_article.php?id=7418

Dunn, James D. G. Jesus, Paul and the Law: Studies in Mark and Galatians. Louisville: Westminster/John Knox, 1990.

_____. Jesus and the Spirit: A Study of the Religious and Charismatic Experience of Jesus and the First Christians as Reflected in the New Testament. Philidelphia: Westminster Press, 1975.

_____. The Theology of Paul the Apostle. Grand Rapids: Wm. B. Eerdmans Publishing Co., 1998.

Enns, Peter. Inspiration and Incarnation: Evangelicals and the Problem of the Old Testament. Grand Rapids: Baker Academic, 2005.

Fitzmyer, Joseph, The Gospel According to Luke, 2 vols. Anchor Bible 28 & 28a. Garden City, NY: Doubleday, 1985.

Fretheim, Terence E. "God and Violence in the Old Testament." Word & World 24.1 (2004), 18–28.

Girard, René. I See Satan Fall Like Lightning. Maryknoll: Orbis, 2001.

_____. Things Hidden Since the Foundation of the World. Stanford University Press: Stanford, 1987.

Gorman, Michael J., Cruciformity: Paul's Narrative Spirituality of the Cross. Grand Rapids: Eerdmans, 2001.

_____. Inhabiting the Cruciform God: Kenosis, Justification, and Theosis in Paul's Narrative Soteriology. Grand Rapids: Eerdmans, 2009.

_____. Reading Revelation Responsibly: Uncivil Worship and Witness: Following the Lamb into the New Creation. Eugene, Or.: Cascade, 2011.

Grenz, Stanley. Renewing the Center: Evangelical Theology in a Post-Theological Era. Grand Rapids: Baker Academic, 2000.

Greven, Philip J., Jr. Spare the Child: The Religious Roots of Punishment and the Psychological Impact of Physical Abuse. New York: Knopf, 1991.

Grogan, Geoffrey W. Two Horizons Old Testament Commentary: Psalms. Grand Rapids: Eerdmans, 2008.

Jenkins, Philip. Laying Down the Sword: Why We Can't Ignore the Bible's Violent Verses. New York: HarperOne, 2011.

Jeremias, Joachim. New Testament Theology. New York: Charles Scribner & Sons, 1971.

Johnson, Sylvester. "New Israel, New Canaan: The Bible, the People of God, and the American Holocaust." Union Seminary Quarterly Review 59, no. 1–2 (2005), 25–39.

Hardin, Michael. The Jesus Driven Life: Reconnecting Humanity with Jesus. Lancaster: JDL Press, 2010.

Hays, Richard. Echoes of Scripture in the Letters of Paul. New Haven: Yale University Press, 1989.

_____. The Moral Vision of the New Testament: Community, Cross, New Creation, A Contemporary Introduction to New Testament Ethics. San Francisco: HarperSanFrancisco, 1996.

H.J. Bruins and J. van der Plicht. "Tell es-Sultan (Jericho): Radiocarbon results of short-lived cereal and multiyear charcoal samples from the end of the Middle Bronze Age" Radiocarbon 37/2 (1995), 213–20.

Hubbard, Robert L. Jr. "Ai" in Bill T. Arnold, H. G. M. Williamson (eds.) Dictionary of the Old Testament: Historical Books (Downers Grove: Intervarsity, 2005), 21–22.

_____. Joshua: The NIV Application Commentary. Grand

Rapids: Zondervan, 2009.

Kraybill, J. Nelson. Apocalypse and Allegiance: Worship, Politics and Devotion in the Book of Revelation. Brazos, 2010.

Kuhn, Karl Allen. Having Words with God: The Bible as Conversation. Minneapolis: Fortress Press, 2008.

Laytner, Anson. Arguing with God: A Jewish Tradition. Northvale, NJ: Jason Aronson Inc., 1990.

Loader, William. Jesus and the Fundamentalism of His Day. Grand Rapids: Eerdmans, 2001.

Marshall, Christopher D., Beyond Retribution: A New Testament Vision for Justice, Crime, and Punishment. Grand Rapids: Eerdmans, 2001.

_____. "The Violence of God and the Hermeneutics of Paul." in Alain Epp Weaver and Gerald J. Mask (eds.) The Work of Jesus Christ in Anabaptist Perspective: Essays in Honor of J. Denny Weaver. Telford: Cascadia, 2008.

Marshall, I. Howard, The Gospel of Luke: A Commentary on the Greek Text. Grand Rapids: Eerdmans, 1978.

Miles, Jack, Christ: A Crisis in the Life of God. New York: Vintage Books, 2001.

McLaren, Brian D. A New Kind of Christianity: Ten Questions That Are Transforming the Faith. San Francisco: HarperOne, 2010.

Myers, Ched. Binding the Strongman: A Political Reading of Mark's Story of Jesus. Maryknoll, NY: Orbis, 1988.

Neville, David J. A Peaceable Hope: Contesting Violent Eschatology in New Testament Narratives. Grand Rapids: Baker Academic, 2013.

_____. "Faithful, True, Violent? Christology and 'Divine Vengeance' in the Revelation of John." in Grimsrud, Ted and Hardin, Michael (eds.). Compassionate Eschatology: The Future as Friend. Eugene, Or.: Cascade, 2011.

Niditch, Susan. War in the Hebrew Bible: A Study in the Ethics of Violence. Oxford, Oxford University Press, 1995.

Nolan, Albert. Jesus Before Christianity. Maryknoll: Orbis Books, 1999.

Noll, Mark A. The Civil War as a Theological Crisis (The Steven and Janice Brose Lectures in the Civil War Era). Chapel Hill: University of North Carolina Press, 2006.

Origen. De Principiis in Alexander Roberts and James Donaldson (eds.). Ante-Nicene Fathers, vol. 4. Edinburgh: T. & T. Clark, 1868.

Origen, Homilies on Joshua in Barbara J. Bruce (Tr.) Cynthia White (Ed.) The Fathers of the Church: A New Translation, vol. 105, Origen: Homilies on Joshua. Washington D.C., Catholic University of America Press, 2002.

Ortberg, John, Stepping Out in Faith: Life-Changing Examples from the History of Israel. Grand Rapids: Zondervan, 2003.

Pascal, Blaise. Pensées (#894) in W. F. Trotter (Tr), Pensées / The Provincial Letters. New York: Random House, 1941.

Peters, F . E. Jerusalem: The Holy City in the Eyes of Chroniclers, Visitors, Pilgrims, and Prophets from the Days of Abraham to the Beginnings of Modern Times. Princeton, NJ: Princeton University Press, 1985.

Pew Center on the States. "State of Recidivism: The Revolving Door of America's Prisons." Washington, DC: The Pew

Charitable Trusts, April 2011.

Schwager, Raymund, Must There Be Scapegoats?: Violence and Redemption in the Bible. San Francisco: Harper & Row, 1987.

Seibert, Eric A. Disturbing Divine Behavior: Troubling Old Testament Images of God. Minneapolis: Fortress, 2009.

_____. The Violence of Scripture. Minneapolis: Fortress, 2012.

Siegel, Daniel J. Mindsight: The New Science of Personal Transformation. New York: Bantam Books, 2011.

Smith, Christian, The Bible Made Impossible: Why Biblicism Is Not a Truly Evangelical Reading of Scripture. Grand Rapids: Brazos, 2012.

Solzhenitsyn, Aleksandr, The Gulag Archipelago. New York, Harper Perennial Modern Classics, 2002.

Stark, Thom. The Human Faces of God: What Scripture Reveals when it Gets God Wrong (and Why Inerrancy Tries to Hide It). Eugene: Wipf & Stock, 2011.

Stassen, Glen. Just Peacemaking: Transforming Initiatives for Justice and Peace. Louisville: Westminster/John Knox, 1998.

Stephan, Maria J. and Erica Chenoweth. "Why Civil Resistance Works." International Security, 33:1 (Summer 2008), 7–44.

Swartley, Willard M., Covenant of Peace: The Missing Peace in New Testament Theology and Ethics. Downers Grove: Eerdmans, 2006.

Swartz, Sunny. Dreams from the Monster Factory: A Tale of Prison, Redemption, and One Woman's Fight to Restore Justice to All. New York: Scribner, 2009.

Tacitus, Annals 15.44. Alfred John Church and William Jackson Brodribb (trans.), The Complete Works of Tacitus. New York: McGraw-Hill,1964, 380–81.

Thorsten, Don, The Wesleyan Quadrilateral: Scripture, Tradition, Reason, & Experience as a Model of Evangelical Theology. Lexington: Emeth Press, 2005.

Tripp, Tedd. Shepherding a Child's Heart, 2nd ed. Wapwallopen, PA: Shepherd, 2005.

Volf, Miroslav. Exclusion and Embrace: A Theological Exploration of Identity, Otherness, and Reconciliation. Nashville: Abindon Press, 1996.

Walvoord, John F. and Zuck, Roy B. (eds.). Bible Knowledge Commentary: Old Testament. Colorado Springs: David C. Cook, 1984.

Warrior, Robert Allan. "Canaanites, Cowboys and Indians." Christianity and Crisis 49 (1989), 261–65.

Webb, William. Corporal Punishment in the Bible: A Redemption Movement-Hermeneutic for Troubling Texts. Downers Grove: IVP Academic, 2011.

_____. in Meadors, Gary T. (Ed.). Four Views on Moving Beyond the Bible to Theology. Grand Rapids: Zondervan, 2009.

_____. Slaves Women and Homosexuals: Exploring the Hermeneutics of Cultural Analysis. Downers Grove: IVP Academic, 2001.

Wright, NT. What Saint Paul Really Said: Was Paul of Tarsus the Real Founder of Christianity? Grand Rapids: Wm. B. Eerdmans, 1997.

Yoder, John Howard. The Politics of Jesus. Grand Rapids: Wm.

265

B. Eerdmans, 1994.

Yoder Neufeld. Thomas R., Killing Enmity: Violence and the New Testament. Grand Rapids: Baker, 2011.

Zehr, Howard. Changing Lenses: A New Focus for Crime and Justice. Scottdale, PA: Herald, 2005.

26485599R00186

Made in the USA
Middletown, DE
30 November 2015